The Art of

Being a Brilliant Teacher

(Read. Do. Inspire.)

Gary Toward, Chris Henley
& Andy Cope

Balloonview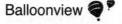

Published by Balloon View Ltd, www.balloonview.com

Printed and bound in Great Britain by
CPI Group (UK) Ltd, Croydon, CR0 4YY

ISBN 978-1-907798-46-7

Foreword

By Richard Gerver

'To teach is to touch a life forever.' This is the motto that greets me every morning when I sit at my desk. It is the same motto that has sat on my desk every day, wherever my desk has been, for the last twenty years. It is a motto that is etched on the bottom of a plastic photo frame, given to me in July 1992 by a child in my first ever class... Funny, you never forget your first class, and what is really weird is that those children remain frozen in time, don't they? I mean, that child will now be an adult in their thirties, possibly with children of their own. Now I feel old!

Back to the motto... I would look at that photo frame, that motto, when I needed a lift; maybe after a difficult meeting with a parent, a challenging conversation with my Head or a tough time with an inspector. It would always bring me back to the reason for my job, the reason for getting out of bed on that cold, wet winter's morning: the children.

I left my life as a teacher four years ago and I miss it every day. Funnily enough, I have realised in that time that the motto was not just about the kids - teaching has touched my life forever. Sometimes it may not feel like it, but it is the greatest job on earth; it is a privilege, an honour, a joy!

In my career I have worked with and met thousands of teachers, most of them driven, dynamic, dedicated professionals, with a passion for their jobs and the children they teach. Sometimes, though, you meet jaded people, people whose flames seem to have been dampened. They usually sit in the beige chair at the back right-hand corner of the staff room, under the union poster that advertises an area meeting that takes place on 3 February 1987! They seek solace in their mug, the one with the chipped handle that was given to them as a freebie by that firm that sells ring binders, a proud trophy from the one time they made it to The Education Show. It would be easy to condemn these colleagues, these un-dead, zombie teachers, but the truth is, they didn't choose to teach because they wanted to screw up kids' lives, they don't get out of bed in the mornings excited about doing a bad job; somewhere, at some time, these sorry souls had wanted to teach, to enlighten, to seek the smile on a student's face as they helped them overcome a challenge or realise a new goal.

Like it or not, teaching is about human interaction, it is about the transference of energy, enthusiasm, passion and learning; to be brilliant teachers we must be brilliant people, in the children's eyes at least. We must learn to nurture these characteristics in ourselves, to value and fiercely protect them. Our job is a selfless one, where we often set our own wellbeing below that of others.

I love this book; I love the fact that the Doctor of Happiness, Andy Cope, has come together with two real-life, amazing educators, Gary Toward and Chris Henley, to cook up this mix of positive self-indulgence just for teachers.

My advice? Stick on a brew - for God's sake don't use the ring binder mug with the chipped handle at the back of the cupboard - find a comfy chair and let yourself escape into *The Art of Being a Brilliant Teacher*. Don't feel guilty about it. The marking can wait!

Truth is, if to teach is to touch a life forever, you'd better start with your own, and now!

Be brilliant!

Richard Gerver - July 2012

Richard Gerver is an award-winning former headteacher, bestselling author and world-renowned speaker, who devotes his life to sharing his passion for the human aspects of leadership, education, change and innovation. His personal motto is: LIVE, LEARN and LAUGH. In reality, to his wife and kid, he is just the embarrassing bloke with the big mouth!

Introduction

A very warm welcome to The Art of Being a Brilliant Teacher. We're delighted you've got this far.

Bad news first: our publisher tells us that there are about 400 million books bought in the UK every year. The 'self-help' percentage is tiny. And the 'teacher self-help' section doesn't actually exist!

But there is a glimmer of hope. One in three people admit to having bought a book 'to look clever'.[1] So, here's our hope: that you might be the one in three, and you leaf through The Art of Being a Brilliant Teacher and something captures your attention. It might cause you to chuckle or think. Or you might identify with one of the stories. You might realise that it's a bit different from what you expected. And you accidentally keep reading. And kind of enjoy it! And leave it lying around in the staffroom.

Our aim is simply to build a comprehensive and entertaining resource that is 'essential reading' for those who are interested in improving their classroom craft. It's a no-nonsense book that is split into four sections:

- Part 1 deals with the context of teaching - the 'busyness' and hurly burly of the profession, making the point that, yes, it's exhausting, but the long holidays are there to compensate! We explore the new science of positive psychology and flourishing, and introduce very simple concepts that will make a difference to you in

---

[1] 67.94% of statistics are made up on the spot.

and out of work. Our thinking is: 'Let's get you sorted first. Then we can help you sort out the kids!'

- Part 2 looks at the art of teaching itself: lesson planning, the learning environment and the starter, main course and pudding of a lesson. We also look at possibly the most important element of teaching - your terms of engagement!

- In part 3 we grapple with the subject of discipline; a subject of massive significance and the most difficult part of the job. It is the main cause of burnout and stress, as well as being the biggest reason for teachers leaving the profession. Yet discipline is generally swept under the carpet. We don't pretend to have all the answers, but we believe we have some simple strategies that will help.

- And we conclude with a short section, Part 4, that brings it all together in one cohesive mass of interconnectedness[2]. Put the pieces together and you have an antidote to teacher training; an 'everything you wish teacher training had covered but didn't'.

Before we start in earnest, we offer two questions for your consideration:

1. First, what do you think parents reply when asked what they want for their own children? Unsurprisingly, their answers are, in priority order, 'happiness', 'confidence', 'a great life', 'satisfaction', 'contentment', 'health' and 'security'.

---

[2] Don't worry folks, this is the only big word in the book!

2. And second, what do schools teach? The same parents answer: 'thinking skills', 'maths', 'subjects', 'literacy' and 'test-taking'.

There appears to be no overlap at all. We're teaching kids how to be successful in 'subjects' in the hope that they get a good job and achieve the things in list one. As Martin Seligman says, 'Schools pave the boulevard toward adult work'.

This book goes beyond 'subjects'. We want you to help pave the boulevard to flourishing children and, as such, we ask you to consider the concept of 'positive education'.

As it says on the cover, read, do and inspire!

Part 1

The context

This section kicks us off with some scene setting. We set out our reasoning behind the book. Who are Chris, Gary and Andy? Why did we write it? And, crucially, why should you read it? We look at teaching as a career and argue that, on the whole, it's got the potential to be the most magnificent job in the world. At least, it has on a good day! So, this part examines what you can do to have more good days. We explore the science of positive psychology and suggest some key habits that will change your life for the better. So, in Part 1 you can forget about teaching. It's really about you!

1. **Why read this book?**

2. **'Busyness'**

3. **Why teach?**

4. **Let the force be with you**

5. **Being brilliant**

Chapter 1

Why read this book?

> *Logic will take you from A to B. Imagination will take you everywhere.*
>
> **Albert Einstein**

In a nutshell

This chapter sets out our stall. We desperately want you to read this book, not to make us fabulously wealthy[3], but to help you become an even better educator. But why should you read it? You're too busy, for one thing! This short introduction sets out our very simple philosophy, our aims and why we have chosen the writing style that we have. We set out the book's uniqueness. And, let's face it, there aren't many books that explore *The Waltons* and *Jeremy Kyle* in the first chapter!

You might like to think of this book as 'everything you wanted to know about teaching but never dared ask'. It's pretty much a pick-and-mix cornucopia of all of the things we feel teachers *should* know. Actually, let's rephrase that. It's what we think *super-teachers* should know.

We sincerely hope you enjoy it. We desperately hope you apply some of it. Or all of it! Adapt it.

---

[3] If we accidentally become rich beyond our wildest dreams, then so be it.

Tweak it. Think of it as a 'cocktail mixer' or 'wine tasting' method of becoming a brilliant teacher. And the payback? Being able to go to work every day and enjoy the profession that you have trained so hard for. When things are going well, it has to be one of the best jobs in the world!

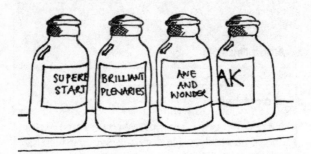

We set out to write a book that meets several needs. First, we want to encourage you to grab some ideas to help you in your own classroom situation. We don't claim that it's a definitive text and we don't profess to have solutions to all the teaching and learning questions in the world. Rather, what we aim to do is encourage you try out a few different ways of tackling the age-old problem of becoming a brilliant teacher. To use Andy's strap-line, why settle for anything less than being yourself, brilliantly?

We also want to make you think. And we mean really think. About you and your career and the impact you have on children and colleagues. Although this book is aimed at teachers, the first section is actually about life. In the big scheme of your life, teaching is part time; living is your full-time occupation! The trouble with the job of living is that it's not a permanent position, so we want to encourage you to make the most of it while you've got it! In essence, we want to get you excited about living first, and then tackle the challenges of teaching next (and, what you'll realise is that, if you get excited about being alive, the challenges of teaching seem much easier to cope with).

> 'If you think something is missing in your life, it is probably 'you'!'
>
> **Robert Holden**

Plus, we wanted to write a book that all teachers would find useful. Primary, secondary, tertiary; young, less young or, ahem, 'experienced'; in inner cities or posh leafy suburbs. Whatever sector and whatever age group, we want to provide you with some easy wins and top tips. If you're newly qualified and looking for some inspiration, this book is for you. If you're an experienced teacher worn down by the daily grind of the profession, this book is for you. If you're an experienced teacher who's drunk from the fountain of enthusiasm and retained your exuberance and optimism, this book is a reminder that you're drinking the right stuff. Keep supping! This book is for you. Or you may be a senior teacher (even a headteacher) who wants to buy this book and leave it lying around the staffroom in the hope that someone will pick it up and leaf through it. Perhaps you're a teaching assistant? In the modern world, schools are asking more and more of you. This book is for you too. Maybe you're not even a teacher? You might be on teacher training or thinking of joining the profession, in which case this book's absolutely for you.

Our style

> *'Rabbit,' said Pooh to himself. 'I like talking to Rabbit. He talks about sensible things. He doesn't use long, difficult words, like Owl. He uses short, easy words, like "What about lunch?" and "Help yourself, Pooh".'*
>
> **A. A. Milne**

Before we start in earnest, a few points about our writing style.

First, we've deliberately given the book a light touch. If you want a tome on 'emotional literacy' or 'the 8 intelligences' or 'safeguarding children in the 21st century', this is not the book for you. If you want a review of government white papers since 1821, this book's *not* for you! We're coming at this from the point of view that the last thing a busy teacher needs is a whole load of academic twaddle or history of government policy. We haven't set out to rant about how to run schools or how successive governments have tinkered with the education system. We have steered the book towards simplicity, common sense and, fingers crossed, fun. If there's one question this book seeks to help you answer it is, 'How can I be a more effective teacher?'

Second, the book is mostly written in the first person, even sometimes venturing to say 'we'. However, it's actually none of us talking alone. We are interchangeable. And we are not always 100% politically correct! We appreciate that humour is a personal thing. We hope you appreciate that we are trying to get our messages across with as much fun as possible and that you enter into the spirit of what we're trying to do - namely, inject some light-heartedness into a subject that can, at times, be very serious indeed.

Third, we have written the book from a practical viewpoint. Chris and Gary count themselves as veterans of the teaching profession. While many seem to get ground down by the relentless pressures of the job, we've managed to retain an enthusiasm (a zest even!) for teaching, and that's been reflected in the results we've achieved. What we've written is true. We've reflected on the best and worst of our combined sixty years of experience. The advice is tried and tested. It works for us and, while we're not suggesting you lift everything from this book and use it verbatim, we want to pique your interest and tweak your taste buds in trying out some of the techniques. We want you to adapt them to suit you, your classroom and your school environment.

So what about our co-author? Why should you listen to him? He's not even a teacher! Well, strictly speaking, he is a qualified teacher but he escaped at the teacher training stage. No stomach for it apparently! But he went on to learn about positivity, happiness and flourishing and has ended up coming full circle, working with schools to help them raise levels of motivation and aspiration. Although he came back into education with the aim of inspiring children, the irony is that it's often the teachers who need the most help! So, Andy adds a unique perspective. He comes with a wealth of experience in the business and academic world and his job is to make you stop and think about your own behaviours and attitudes.[4]

---

[4] Andy has promised to throw in a few business models too... but he says he won't be offended if you skip those bits!

Fourth, in any school the most important people in it are actually the kids... or should it be the students... or maybe the pupils? We use all of these terms because it's what we say in our job and so will most teachers. 'Kids' are why we come to work and we are proud to say they feature strongly in the following pages.

What planet are we on?

Thankfully, the same planet as you! All three of us are coming at this from a real-world planet earth perspective. We don't live in some happy-clappy land where children skip into school with a grin and an apple for teacher. We don't breathe in the rarefied air of Walton Mountain. Ours is not a rose-tinted world where Jim-Bob stays behind after class to thank you personally. 'And I jolly well enjoyed doing my homework Miss,' he gushes. 'Those quadratic equations were life changing.'

We don't live in an idyllic world where children arrive smart and refreshed, empty vessels that are 'learning ready'. And ours is certainly not a world where every parent attends parents' evening and they queue up to thank you for being the best teacher in the world.

Miss Kent enjoyed the perks of being a super-teacher.

No siree. We have both feet entrenched in modern Britain, where it rains a lot and children don't always value education. Ours is a world where parents often don't turn up at parents' evenings at all! And children sometimes turn up to class unkempt and un-breakfasted. Some of the boys fall asleep because they've been up until 4 a.m. playing X-Box live with kids in Japan. And you get home, sometimes very late, exhausted and grumpy. All you want to do is fall into bed, but you've got some marking and prep to do for tomorrow! When I look out of my window it's not some heavenly scene of white picket fences and perfectly groomed children chattering excitedly about what they're going to learn. When I look out of my window, it's more like a holding pen for a *Jeremy Kyle* show.

And that's why this book is going to be so useful to you. It contains a wealth of information, some obvious, some less so. Some will be new, some will be a gentle reminder. But it's about teaching NOW. Not how it used to be done. If children aren't arriving in your classroom 'learning ready', your job is to make them so. And, to be frank, that's the hardest part.

Our message is that teaching is a demanding profession. But it also has the potential to be the best profession in the world.

Why should you listen to us?

This is a very fair question. Why indeed? Consider this to be the case for the defence!

Andy

Why should teachers listen to what I have to say? Crikey me! Pressure! Well, I do lots of things. I'm quite famous if you're under ten, as my 'Spy Dog' series is doing really well. But that's just a happy accident. I guess it proves I have a mental age of about 8?[5]

I left university and spent a few years working in retail management (that's a posh way of saying I worked at *WHSmith*). I made my fortune (i.e. paid off my loan) and left to do some travelling. I came back to the UK and trained to be a teacher. The aim was to be a secondary school teacher, but my first job offer was from an FE College so I kind of fell into adult education. Loved it! I crept up the career ladder and ended up working in the business development team. Basically, we were the mavericks who were challenged with designing and delivering corporate courses. I spent time teaching at Leicester Uni. I excelled in delivering highfaluting MBA subjects and was always really pleased when I could include so much academia that I'd leave the delegates flummoxed by my cleverness. I loved it. Bizarrely, they loved it too! And I kept getting promoted!

Then, pretty much overnight, I realised I'd been doing it wrong. I discovered a subject called 'positive psychology'. Remember Victor Kiam? He loved his shaver so much he bought the company. I loved the subject so much I did a PhD in it! I bought into it big time. I stumbled across the science of happiness, flourishing and wellbeing. And now that's what I do. I feed my research into my workshops and, hey presto, we have some fab courses that change lives! And the best thing of all... no big words!

I deliver *'The Art of Being Brilliant'* workshops in businesses and schools across the world. Then, one

---

[5] You might have already noticed my liking for Winnie the Pooh? Plenty more to come!

day, I turned up at a school in Leicester and there were two slightly odd teachers called Gary and Chris...

Chris

I have been teaching for thirty years. Put differently, I have taught roughly 30,000 lessons in three different secondary schools, and I have been lucky enough to be given opportunities to teach in primary schools as well. I am a languages teacher originally, but I have also taught drama and English. I was a Head of Department for fifteen years, I have been a Senior Leader developing teaching and learning for eight years and I recently enjoyed a sabbatical year promoting healthy lifestyles in nearly fifty schools nationwide.

I am a passionate believer in the young people of today. The conventional orthodoxy is to denigrate children, teenagers, teachers and schools. Low standards, no discipline... you know the narrative!

I have never yet seen this blackboard jungle in my thirty years. I just don't recognise it. My reflection is of having met and worked with some incredible people, people who have given their hearts and souls to this business of teaching. My view of our young people is that when they are well led, they will bear comparison with any of their forebears. I have mostly found them to be hard working, loyal, well mannered and an absolute credit to their generation when they are well taught by good teachers. Our purpose is to share with future generations of teachers how to make this dream come true.

I am so proud to be a teacher! Those who know me well are kind enough to say I am a good teacher. If I am, then it is not because I am naturally a good teacher. It is because I have worked and worked and worked at the craft of teaching a good lesson!

Gary

I've now worked in seven schools countrywide, with pupils ranging in age from ten to nineteen. This has included being Head or Principal at three schools in Leicestershire, including the Pupil Referral Unit where I worked alongside two other colleagues as Executive Head to lead the facility successfully out of 'special measures'. My spiritual home has been South Wigston High School in Leicestershire, where I have been headteacher for over eleven years and, with the help of many excellent colleagues, moving the school from a 'satisfactory' grade in 2000 to 'outstanding' in 2010. I've never given up teaching and, while I taught Design Technology for my first twelve years in the profession, I have taught most areas on the secondary curriculum since then. Teaching English, however, has become a fantastic experience where I look forward to every lesson. I can't imagine a better job; different every day, people to inspire and people to be inspired by. What a great opportunity we teachers have: to create the classroom conditions (much more about this later - hold your breath) that allow kids to flourish and grow.

Oh, and I also love getting kids to the top of mountains and I run a didgeridoo club on Fridays.

No more evidence your honour

> '*Slumber not in the tents of your fathers! The world is advancing. Advance with it!*'
>
> **Giuseppe Mazzini**

The interesting thing about being a teacher is that you just don't know how much influence you have. It is indeed a huge responsibility to get it right and help influence future generations for the better. Young people often get bad press, usually because of a few bad eggs. From my perspective, despite working with many youngsters who may be defined as 'challenging', it's a privilege to work with young people as, more often than not, they are brilliant.

So, m' Lord, we rest the case for the defence. Collectively, we've got decades of experience behind us and have learned an awful lot from some fantastic practitioners, as well as inventing a few things ourselves. We bring experience from all sectors of education and, with Andy on board, an 'outsider's' view too. We hope you enjoy our ideas and can use a few of them to help you become the best teacher you can be.

Bonus story

Kung Fu Panda... epic story of martial arts, ancient mystical powers, enlightenment and, err, noodle soup?

Our hero is a rather rotund and accident-prone panda. Panda's dad (a bird who owns and runs a noodle outlet... don't ask!) tells him that he feels Panda is ready to take over the running of the shop and that one day he will tell him the way to make his 'Special Ingredient' Noodle Soup.

But Panda is destined for greater things - he travels across China to take on the mantle of the Dragon Warrior, facing pain, tiredness and stamina-sapping physical and mental tests until he is ready to receive the Dragon Scroll. The Scroll is an ancient parchment that is reserved only for viewing by the true Dragon Warrior. He will need its secrets to fight the mighty challenger to his new title.

To his horror, he finds that he cannot read the scroll as there is no writing upon it; no writing means no secret - he must fight the challenger on his own! *Yikes!*

Full of self-doubt, he meets up again with his dad who announces, with some gravity, that he has something to tell his son. Panda listens, hoping to find out how he can be a Panda when his father is a Crane! Instead, his father offers this jaw-dropper, 'Son, there is no special ingredient in the 'Special Ingredient' Noodle Soup. It's just that people believe there is.'

No way!

Equally there is no special secret in the scroll, it is made of reflective paper and reveals, when you look at it, that 'you' are the special ingredient!

(There's a message in there somewhere folks!)

Chapter 2

Busyness

> *We can't stop the waves but we can learn to surf.*
>
> **Jon Kabat Zinn**

In a nutshell

This chapter looks at why we decided to pitch this book at the level of 'brilliant'. It introduces the concepts of 'busyness' and 'destination addiction' and points out that life's too short to be counting down to retirement. We also point out, as politely as possible, that us oldies complaining about the 'yoof of today' is probably a whinge passed down from the ancients! Andy tells his pop-tastic factory story and we check out the concept of continuous improvement. We finish off the chapter with a reminisce about the good old days of teaching, before political correctness had been invented.

Our publisher advised that some people might find the book title a little pretentious. But we stuck to our guns. I mean, what did he expect us to call it? *Being an Average Teacher? Or, The Teacher's Survival Guide or, Achieving Mediocrity in the Classroom?*

What's the point? We want you to pitch in at 'world class'.

If you're just entering the profession, or already established, why wouldn't you aspire to be the best teacher you could possibly be? The influence you have is profound, so our view is that you should strive to make it as positive as possible. And, this book is bigger than your subject. It's about you! We can all think of teachers who know their subject inside out but are failing to engage the students.

Many things have changed in teaching over the last thirty or forty years. Successive governments have constantly tinkered with the curriculum, inspection regimes, hours of working, funding methods and, of course, even the name of the government department responsible for it all! Initiatives have come and gone. If you've got enough teaching miles under your belt you will have experienced that déjà vu feeling as the same initiatives come around again and again!

What hasn't changed, though, is that every year another cohort of kids turns up for teachers to inspire. A sea of faces. A babble of first-day noise. A classroom full of nervous excitement, in anticipation of the year ahead. Chris and Gary, even after umpteen years, still get a buzz before these days. We want you to have that feeling, every year... your own feeling of anticipation of a new opportunity to inspire and enthuse kids in their own learning.

New year's revolution

> *There is more to life than increasing its speed.*
>
> **Mahatma Ghandi**

Some teachers get excited about the start of the new year. Others sigh, heavy-heartedly, 'Here we go again!' We call this 'destination addiction', and it's rife in education. 'Destination addiction' suggests that, subconsciously, most teachers' primary objective is to 'get through the week' or 'survive until half term'. In fact, I've never met a teacher who doesn't know exactly how many weeks until the next half term.[6]

Essentially, what many teachers are doing is counting down, wishing their weeks away.[7] The more you think about this the more ridiculous it is. I call it 'stinking thinking'. Let's not pull any punches. Nobody (even if you're a fresh-faced NQT reading this book) has enough weeks left on this planet to waste them by counting down. We're wishing our lives away! Our take is that life is a short and precious gift.

We understand why teachers can get stuck in the habit of counting down to half term, but our belief is that we can learn better mental habits. There are ways of thinking that can elevate us from the energy-sapping mediocrity of 'destination addiction'. So, our aim is not merely to give you fresh ideas to spice up your classroom craft, but to help you lose some bad habits of thinking that you might have inadvertently gathered along the way. What if you could *unlearn* these bad habits and *relearn* some cool new ways of thinking? This would rejuvenate you in and out of work.

---

[6] I've met some who know it to the nearest hour and minute!

[7] During my teaching practice I spent some time with a nearly retired Economics lecturer. He had the acronym DILLIGAF on the wall. I asked him what it meant. He replied that it was his motto, 'Do I Look Like I Give A F***'.

So, I guess one of the pertinent questions is, why do we get stuck in 'destination addiction'? Why does a teacher's energy ebb away? I suppose we could blame the usual suspects - restructures, budget cuts, syllabus changes, Ofsted, lazy colleagues, pension changes, management, marking, government, planning, society, parents, 'initiatives' or, classically, the *kids* (or, as Andy likes to call them our 'customers'!).

You could go back through the ages and find that there have always been exactly the same moans and groans about children that we have today: unruly, rude, loud, scruffy, ill mannered, disrespectful. Even the ancients were concerned about the 'youth of today':

> *The children now love luxury; they have bad manners, contempt for authority; they show disrespect for elders and love chatter in place of exercise. Children are now tyrants, not the servants of their households. They no longer rise when elders enter the room. They contradict their parents, chatter before company, gobble up dainties at the table, cross their legs and tyrannise their teachers.*
>
> **Socrates, 469-399 BC**

Some interesting words from an old master. (But what are dainties we wonder?)

Miss Grimthorpe had a stormy relationship with her class.

So it seems then that teachers always have been, and probably always will be, faced with a challenge. It's simply because kids are growing up, pushing, prodding and stepping over boundaries. Many will arrive from homes where there is little structure, weak guidance and unhelpful role models, so they will need even more support and investment. For another group, school will be the one constant in an ever-changing and unstable home life.

The role of the teacher has hardly changed though. When that door closes and it's you and thirty young people, it's much the same as it has always been. It can be terrifying, exciting, hilarious, inspirational, depressing or exhilarating (or all of these things - a typical drama lesson for Chris, apparently!).

Teaching is a crucial role, but also one that often receives criticism. In many respects this criticism unites the two sides of the coin, teacher and learner. It almost seems like a yearly rite of passage now for teenagers and teachers together to pick up newspapers or turn on the news at the end of the summer to find that exams must be getting easier because more kids are passing them.

How rude!

Let's apply the thinking to another industry to prove how faulty it is. The principle of 'Kaizen' or 'continuous improvement' has existed in car manufacturing for decades. Have you noticed that the quality of cars keeps improving? Andy's has got 100,000 miles on the clock and has never caused him a problem. Nobody seems to be arguing that we're just lowering the way we measure car quality. Other industries seem to accept, without question, that methods have improved.

So, have our media colleagues ever thought that maybe, just maybe, teaching has improved significantly over the last few decades and pupils have been responding to it? We know many headteachers across the country who tell us that the new teachers joining the profession are arriving better prepared and equipped than ever before to face the rigours and challenges ahead.

Good old days?

One headteacher gave a classic example of just how much things have changed since he was on teaching practice in 1980. Can you imagine how much hell would break loose in the press if the following event happened in a modern classroom?

I walked into the workshop to find a boy spread-eagled across the work bench. His hands had been firmly gripped in metalworking vices each side of him and his feet held in the same manner below. The teacher, a fearsome sight, was circling the boy, berating him for his poor behaviour. The lesson started and the class worked around the unfortunate student for nearly an hour before he was released and allowed to leave with the others.

An interesting approach, eh? Although we do accept that some readers might sigh wistfully and hark back to 'the good old days' when this kind of discipline and horseplay was the norm, we are fairly sure that there are more practical and humane methods of managing your classroom.

We want every teacher to be brilliant, to be an inspiring force in the classroom and to produce the best learners they possibly can. While we're not naive enough to believe this book will magically transform teachers into Third Dan grand masters of teaching, we have aimed to decant into it the thoughts and collected wisdom of a range of outstanding performers we've met over three decades. All of the advice and guidance we give has been used and is still used by high-level practitioners in classrooms around the country.

Pop-tastic?

Andy tells the story of when he ran his 'Art of Being Brilliant' workshop for a very famous drinks manufacturer. He had forty production managers on the course, all male. His ice-breaker was, 'What brings you joy at work guys? What gives you that *Ready Brek* glow?'

The delegates showed no hesitation. They leaped out of their seats. 'Breaking the production record,' they shouted, punching the air in delight. 'We are the most efficient factory in Europe. Do you know what Andy? We can produce half a million cans of pop every day...'.

So it's clear that whatever your job is, doing it well will make you feel good. And imagine how much greater the satisfaction when you consider that teaching is about producing human beings. Not in a mass produced identikit kind of way, but in a procession of unique children who will, in one way or another, make their mark on the world. And you get to shape them. Is there anything more important that you will ever do?

Hidden treasures

> *To think creatively, we must be able to look afresh at what we normally take for granted.*
>
> **Johann Wolfgang Von Goethe**

This book isn't about throwing out the baby with the bathwater. The chances are, you are already an excellent teacher! We want you to consider alternative ways of doing things and to tap into the resources that you already hold. In short, we want to make your life easier!

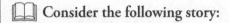

Consider the following story:

An old beggar had been sitting by the side of the road for many years. One day a stranger walked up to him. 'Spare some change?' the beggar asked, optimistically holding out a faded old baseball cap.

'I have nothing to give you,' replied the stranger, *'but... what is that you're sitting on?'* he mused.

'It's nothing,' replied the beggar, 'it's just an old box; I've been sitting on it for as long as I can remember.'

'What's inside it?' asked the stranger.

'Nothing,' replied the beggar, 'it's empty... I think.'

'So, you've never looked inside it?' queried the stranger. 'Why not have a look?'

'There doesn't seem much point,' replied the beggar, but nevertheless, he got up and bent over the box and, after some initial struggling, managed to prise off the lid.

To his astonishment, the box was filled with gold!

A few questions spring to mind, such as:

- What box have you been sitting on without realising it?

- What 'treasure' might you find if you opened it?

- What hidden qualities do you have that you've been taking for granted?

- What if you already have all the resources you need? What if they're already inside you, ready to be discovered?

Top tips

1. Get excited about the start of the new school year.

2. Appreciate that life's too short to wish the weeks away.

3. Speak highly of your job to family and friends. Speak highly of children. Be proud to be a teacher.

4. Appreciate that in thirty years' time, when you reflect on your life, these will be 'the good old days'.

Bonus story

All three of us love to see the funny side of teaching. And, it's hard not to look back at the 'olden days' with a nod of appreciation. Maybe a teacher's life really was easier? This email did the rounds a few months ago so we thought we'd share it with you. It's entitled '1970 v 2010'.

Scenario 1:

Johnny and Mark get into a fistfight after school:

1970 - Crowd gathers. Johnny wins. Johnny and Mark shake hands and end up best mates for life.

2010 - Police called, arrest Johnny and Mark. Charge them with assault, both expelled even though Mark started it. Both children go to anger management programs for three months. School Governors hold a meeting to implement bullying prevention programs.

Scenario 2:

Robbie won't keep still in class, disrupts other students.

1970 - Robbie sent to office and given six of the best by the Headmaster. Returns to class, sits still and does not disrupt class again.

2010 - Robbie given huge doses of Ritalin. Becomes a zombie. Tested for ADHD. Robbie's parents get fortnightly disability payments and school gets extra funding from state because Robbie has a disability.

Scenario 3:

Johnny takes apart leftover firecrackers from Guy Fawkes' night, puts them in a model Airfix paint bottle, blows up an ants' nest.

1970 - Ants die.

2010 - Police, armed forces and anti-terrorism squad called. Johnny charged with domestic terrorism, MI5 investigate parents, siblings removed from home, computers confiscated. Johnny's dad goes on a terror watch list and is never allowed to fly again.

Chapter 3

Why teach?

Wealth is what you have left when all your money's run out.

Roger Hamilton

In a nutshell

In this chapter we make the case that the job is a toughie but that the pay, although not in the banking category, is actually not too bad. We ask you to consider alternative ways of measuring your wealth. We take a peek at the evolution of 'bad' and 'good' and explain that they don't weigh the same. We introduce you to the weird world of NLP and explain that there's no such thing as 'reality' - we simply filter the world around us to make sense of things, but what we're experiencing is distorted, generalised and sometimes deleted![8]

Being a teacher is not an easy job. We could argue that it's more challenging than ever before as performance management systems and school league tables mean that teachers can no longer hide. But with the hard work come great rewards.

---

[8] Don't worry, we are not suggesting that there is some Matrix-style 'parallel universe', but we do want to introduce you to some stuff that is genuinely interesting and will challenge your current thinking.

How many jobs are there where people are given the power and tools to change lives on a daily basis?

As Ginott said:

> I've come to the frightening conclusion that I am the decisive element in the classroom. It's my daily mood that makes the weather. As a teacher, I possess a tremendous power to make a child's life miserable or joyous. I can be a tool of torture or an instrument of inspiration. I can humiliate or humour, hurt or heal. In all situations, it is my response that decides whether a crisis will be escalated or de-escalated and a child humanized or de-humanized.

Ginott, 1972

True, there are those who should not be in the profession and have found themselves in a job with a group of people with whom they have little empathy. However, most teachers go to work each day to make a difference. The average teacher in a secondary school might teach at least one subject to five different groups of around thirty pupils each week and have responsibility for the pastoral care of a further thirty. Multiply that total of one hundred and eighty pupils by forty years and you find that in their career many teachers will have had the opportunity to influence over 7000 young people.

> 'And I know it seems easy,' said Piglet to himself, 'but it isn't everyone who could do it.'
>
> **A. A. Milne**

Without doubt teachers have ups and downs. The kids aren't always easy. There's a lot of baggage brought in to schools; a wide variety of home-related problems, from abuse to separated parents, or those with no parents, or parents who have low literacy or low income. Many schools have a great spectrum of pupils, from those whose parents are millionaires to those whose parents are on the breadline.

As we have found out, there are many rewards, but none so great as finding that the pupils respect you, and are loyal to you and the school. Teachers often bump into past pupils, many of whom may not have been easy and would, no doubt, have had the odd tongue-lashing. Typically they will shake a teacher's hand, smile and be pleased to see them. Often they will say things like, 'I was a little bugger wasn't I, Miss?' The use of 'Sir' and 'Miss' seems to die hard, and twenty-somethings will still greet their old teachers using these terms. In fact, recently we heard of an association of past pupils and teachers of a school where octogenarian ex-pupils and even older ex-teachers had only just managed to get around to first name terms!

A wide variety of parents exist in our world and it is they that really hold the power. While teachers can influence life from the classroom, it's parents who influence most of the long-term development. We've come across abusive parents, parents who nurture learning at home, parents who are unsupportive and parents who are very supportive. Just as we rarely tell the bus driver that he's done a great job driving through that traffic, it is rare that teachers are congratulated by parents. It's our job and parents take it for granted that we should do it well. On the other hand, we'd be straight on to the poor old bus driver if he'd braked too hard and caused our shopping to scatter down the aisle of the bus. Similarly, in teaching, it's easy for parents to give the teacher who has given their son a detention for poor behaviour a hard time, especially when the son in question has not explained the full reason for the punishment. However, most teachers understand the rules and accept this as 'part of the job', graciously taking the plaudits when they do come and reflecting wisely on those who knock them.

So why teach? Is it the pay? Well, it's not bad and comparatively much better than it was in the early 1980s. You'll not become staggeringly rich though. At least, not in monetary terms. In our view, you will become staggeringly wealthy in the widest sense of the term. You will have enriched kids' lives; their loyalty, their honesty and their warmth will have astounded you. Every now and then something will happen that will remind you that what you do has had a dramatic and positive impact on someone. And you'll be proud to be a teacher!

Light bulbs

Those light-bulb moments come out of the blue. Take Billy, for example. Billy was a bright lad, working well above the expected norm for his age group. At the age of fourteen he had resisted all attempts by a wide variety of teachers over the years to persuade him to have higher aspirations. Billy wanted to have an easy life and stroll into a job with little challenge. Billy's light-bulb moment came on a school visit to Paris. While walking up the *Champs Elysées* Billy tugged at his group leader's arm and said, 'How do I get to be a teacher? I want to do what you do and inspire kids like this.' Now that's why teachers teach! It has nothing to do with the fact that Billy wanted to become a teacher. It was the simple fact that one teacher had unlocked the door to a talented young man possibly realising his potential.

Skool funnies

> *A business has to be involving, it has to be fun, and it has to exercise your creative instincts.*
>
> **Richard Branson**

Even the moments of seeming madness can make you glad to do the job. In their career, most teachers will have plenty of chuckles over misunderstandings by their pupils. Check out these exam funnies, taken from an article in the Daily Mail:

Chemistry

Q: What is nitrate?

A: *It is much cheaper than a day rate.*

Q: Give a brief explanation of the meaning of the term 'hard water'.

A: *Ice*

Biology

Q: What is a fibula?

A: *A little lie*

Q: What is the meaning of the word 'VARICOSE'?

A: *Close by*

Q: What does 'terminal illness' mean?

A: *When you become ill at the airport.*

Maths

Q: A new car costs £32,000. It is expected to depreciate 12% each year for 4 years and then depreciate 8% each year thereafter. Find the value of the car in 6 years.

A: *No one will drive cars in 6 years with fuel going up like it is.*

History

Q: What did Mahatma Gandhi and Genghis Khan have in common?

A: *Unusual names*

Q: What is Karl Marx known for?

A: *Karl Marx was one of the Marx brothers.*

Now, of course, in typical British tabloid fashion, the *Mail* is trying to stir up some anti-teenage sentiment. They're using these examples to 'prove' that standards have declined. To balance things up and prove that language has confused us through the ages, check out these gems. From grown-ups! Decades ago! According to Jasper Carrot, these are genuine statements written on car insurance claims forms:

- *I pulled away from the kerb, glanced at my mother-in-law and headed over the embankment.*

- *I'd been driving for forty years when I fell asleep at the wheel and had an accident.*

- *The pedestrian had no idea which direction to run so I ran over him.*

- *I knocked over a man. He admitted it was his fault as he had been run over before.*

So maybe today's generation don't have a monopoly on stupidity. We'll finish with these, from the pensions' office (from adults who were schooled in the 1940s and '50s):

- *In accordance with your instructions, I have given birth to twins in the enclosed envelope.*

- *I want money as quick as you can send it. I have been in bed with my doctor all week and he does not seem to be doing me any good.*

- *Re your enquiry. The teeth in the top are all right, but the ones in my bottom are hurting horribly.*

So this takes us right back to Socrates. The crucial thing all teachers need to grasp is that kids will be kids. They will learn if the climate in the classroom is right and, if not, they will indeed 'gobble up your dainties'... ouch!

Praise be!

As a teacher you will give out plenty of pats on the back, commendations and other forms of praise and, just occasionally, you'll get some too. Treasure them. Whether they come in the form of a card, a letter or an email, treasure them. Keep them in a file or pin them up. After a difficult day, look at them.

Over the years you will build up quite a collection from different sources. These are priceless little reminders of how much you mean to those you teach and those you work with. Not only that, if you bear in mind that we humans are not quick to praise people for doing their job well, the collection you build up will also represent a multitude of silent satisfied customers.

Good v bad

Andy's research can help explain the science of positive versus negative. Thinking about the last twelve months of teaching, which children stick in your mind the most, the good ones or bad ones? Which lesson do you recall the fastest, the dreamy lesson where everything was effortless, or the lesson from the depths of Hades that left you wondering why you entered the profession? You know, that lesson which left you shaking and meant you downed a bottle of Chardonnay when you got home?

Science suggests that you will almost certainly be able to recall the lesson from hell! In terms of positivity, it's useful to know and understand that 'bad' weighs more than 'good'. Let me explain. Throughout evolution, we've learned to be careful. We've survived because we've been cautious. For example, if you hear screeching tyres and a blaring horn, your instinct is to leap out of the way. The feelings of fear and the associated adrenaline rush have saved your life. As a result, we're tuned in to negativity, especially danger, simply because it's a matter of survival of the species. The problem with happiness and joy is that these emotions don't save your life, they merely enrich it. So, subconsciously, we pay less attention to positive emotions. That, folks, is just the way we're programmed.

So what?

Basically, this means that we can get stuck in a negative mindset where we notice the bad kids and fail to notice the brilliant ones! Our attention is naturally drawn to the negative. Andy points out that for the first ten years of his married life he and his wife would go through the ritual of bragging about who'd had the worst day. Louise would invariably go first, telling him in great detail about the terrible behaviour of one particular pupil or about the angry parent who'd phoned her to complain that she'd given Johnny a detention. She'd go on and on about the poor standards of behaviour and the hyper lads who were drinking Red Bull and the fact that she was at the end of her tether. And the truth was, for ten years Andy wasn't even listening. He was merely waiting for his go. As soon as Louise paused for breath he'd be in there: 'You think your day's been bad? Wait till I tell you how bad mine's been!' It was a ten-year competition to see who'd had the worst day! That's just the way it was. But, thankfully (and this is crucial), that's not how it has to be. Andy realised that he loved his job. Why was he coming home and moaning about the one or twp bad pupils, when the other hundred had been fantastic? Bad is stronger than good, that's why.

Ask yourself whether you're focusing on the right things. Maybe a change of perspective will serve you well?

Weird science

> *Just living is not enough. One must have sunshine, freedom and a little flower.*
>
> **Hans Christian Andersen**

I meet very few teachers who have trained in NLP. Neurolinguistic programming is, at its core, the science of how we process information and make sense of the world. It's all about how to build rapport and communicate more effectively so, personally, I think it should be mandatory for all teachers!

Here's a taster. NLP talks of generalisation, distortion and deletion.

- **Generalisation:** Our brains cannot take in everything that goes on around us so, in order to make sense of the world, we generalise. For example, the media tells us that all teenagers are hoodies. What, every single one of them? Or, I've heard teachers say, 'we've got a particularly bad Year 10.' Wow, 250 awful kids. Not a single good one. Amazing!

    Of course, generalisation is useful, that's why we do it. If someone asks, 'How was your day?' they don't want a blow-by-blow minute-by-minute account of every detail. So you generalise. 'It was fine thanks.' Or, if someone asks how you're feeling, the last thing they want to hear is, 'I'm feeling like a 6 out of 10. Lungs and respiratory system are functioning very well. Slight pain in my left knee from gardening. Self-esteem is suffering because one of the kids said I looked "haggard" last week and, to be honest, it's made me look closely at my wrinkles. I've got a bit of wind too if you really want to know. Nothing major, just a bit bloated. I think it was those mushy peas? The athlete's foot on my right foot is worse than it was yesterday and my piles are playing up.'

Thankfully, we sum it up as, 'not too bad, considering'.

- **Distortion:** Typically, teachers complain about 'the class from hell where nothing went right.' Sure, it might have been a tough lesson, but, on careful reflection, you might find that some of it went very well and that some of the kids learned loads. Your brain has a terrific piece of kit called a reticular activating system. Your RAS acts as a filter. You are bombarded with so much information that it's impossible to take everything in, so your RAS sifts it, bringing to your attention what it thinks is most important to you. So, for example, if you're thinking of buying a new car you start to notice new cars. Your RAS keeps pointing them out. 'Another Mini Cooper. Nice colour too. Go on, you know you want one!'

A lesson for life is that, generally speaking, you get what you focus on. Too many people are filtering out the good stuff and focusing instead on the bad weather, unruly kids and excessive workload. Here's a real example of a checkout lady I encountered at Morrisons.[9] As she scanned my items I commented in a passing-the-time-of-day way that it was a glorious day for the time of year. She stopped scanning for a microsecond, looked at me and said, 'Is it dear? I only ever see the rain.'

Be careful what you focus on folks! It affects your physiology and psychology - massively!

---

[9] For some reason 'Morrisons' doesn't have an apostrophe. As a paid-up member of the 'apostrophe police' I choose, where possible, to shop at the grammatically superior 'Sainsbury's'.

- As for **deletion**, try this one; count the number of Fs in this sentence:

  FINISHED FILES ARE THE RESULT OF YEARS OF SCIENTIFIC STUDY COMBINED WITH THE EXPERIENCE OF YEARS.[10]

Point made? Most people will count 3 Fs, discounting 3 that are actually there! Some information is just deleted. Your brain deems it superfluous and therefore refuses to see it.

Too many teachers generalise, distort and delete to create a world in which teaching is a hellish existence and schools are populated entirely by demonic young people. This also applies outside of a school context. For example, my father-in-law lives in a tabloid world where the NHS kills people, every foreigner is an illegal immigrant and all footballers earn a billion pounds a week.

Every single day is different in teaching. You might have the same lessons and the same groups of pupils daily, but because you are interacting with developing young people, challenging them to learn, each day brings different experiences and rewards. The school environment and school day are also organic. The timetable, the curriculum, sports days, productions, concerts, parents' evenings and meetings, to name but a few, ebb and flow throughout the year. This may seem to complicate matters, but in fact it adds spice to school life.

A great school has a life beyond the classroom, and these schools are filled with great staff, creating those

---

[10] Count again. There are actually six.

extra learning opportunities and developments that breathe *joie de vivre* into the day. For us, this is the most exciting part of school life. Looking back after you've retired, the chances are you won't remember your Year 10 Maths lesson on a wet Wednesday, or the Year 4s learning their times tables. But you will remember the school play, or when you coached the Year 9s to the regional cup final, or the delight on the face of a Year 11 when she opened her results envelope and had exceeded expectations by a mile. These are the moments. And, if you take a philosophical perspective, we can easily argue that life is just a series of moments. That's all we have! Moment after moment, ticking away. Our advice is to tune in to the good moments a little more. Become aware of the vibe, the buzz, the banter and the energy. When a class is going well, take a few seconds to stand tall and appreciate it. Take a deep breath, smile and survey the scene. You created the environment where this moment occurred. Savour the feeling. Stop letting the negative moments dominate!

The most typical response from trainee or newly qualified teachers when asked, 'Why on earth do you want to get into one of the most stressful professions in the world?' is something which suggests that they quite simply want to make a difference. Is there a better reason? Changing lives for the better is pretty hot stuff. How many professions, apart from maybe doctors and nurses, have such an impact? Not that many. It comes once again back to Ginott. That awesome power of being the weather god of the classroom means that, by getting the seasons right, your pupils will flourish.[11]

---

[11] Oh, and the holidays aren't bad either!

Top tips

1. Keep all thank you or praising cards/notes/emails you are given and pin them up somewhere, so after a hard day you can be reminded how valued you are. Read them often.

2. Savour the brilliant moments in the classroom. People might not send you letters about them but they are significant. Write them down!

3. Focus on the positives, at work and at home.

4. Stop deleting the good stuff!

Bonus poem

> ### Ithaca
> *Always keep Ithaca in your mind.*
> *To arrive there is what you are destined for.*
> *But don't hurry the journey at all.*
> *Better if it lasts for many years.*
> *So you're old by the time you reach the isle.*
> *Wealthy with all you have gained on the way*
> *And not expecting Ithaca to make you rich.*
> *Ithaca gave you the beautiful journey.*
> *Without her you'd never have set out.*
> *But she has nothing more to give you now.*
> *And if you find her poor, Ithaca won't have deceived you.*
> *Wise as you have become after so much experience,*
> *You'll have understood by then what these Ithacas mean.*[12]
> **C. P. Cavafy**

---

[12] Answers on a postcard?

Chapter 4

Let the force be with you

The Future's so Bright, I Gotta Wear Shades

1980s hit for Timbuk 3

In a nutshell

We look at 'mood hoovers', people who get inadvertently trapped in the dark side where every silver lining has a cloud! We examine how this default negativity can sneak up on us, before turning to the antidote. 'Positive psychology' is about inhabiting the bright side, where your heliotropic effect gives life to those in most need. The 2%ers are those weirdos who smile a lot, have bounce, energy, enthusiasm and positivity. We examine (albeit in hugely summarised form) the key habits of the 2%ers.

In almost every staff room lives at least one 'mood hoover'; a term coined by Andy referring to a person who lives on the negative side of life. A bit like Darth Vader, they've moved over to the dark side where there's a lot of heavy breathing and plenty of doom and gloom. You know the sort of person; someone who has seen it all, tried whatever you suggest, can't handle change and, above all, lights up the room when they leave! This is the person who, when you've arrived at school full of the joys of spring, looking forward to the day (even your bottom set, last lesson), tries to suck all positivity out of you when you meet them in the staff room. They'll typically be wallowing in the same seat they always sit in and will have been at the school for some time. Oh yes, they have been there, got the 'victim' tee-shirt and the full set of medals. They have turned into a happiness-sucking machine and if you get in their range you will be targeted: 'Teaching was better in the olden days. Ofsted are out to get us. The school management haven't a clue. The kids are little devils. The parents even worse...'.

There's only one antidote. You must always choose, yes choose, to be a 2%er! So what on earth is a 2%er?

Are you sitting comfortably? No? Well, here goes anyway... I studied psychology as part of my degree and it was interesting stuff. I learned about problems such as depression, paranoia, disorders, anxiety, phobias - in fact, if it could go wrong in your head, we'd learn about it! We read big thick textbooks crammed full of people with problems. And that was fine, because that's what psychology was all about. Fixing people. If there was a scale of wellbeing from +10 (feeling fab) to -10 (totally lousy), traditional strands of psychology had always been about getting people from, say, -9 to 0 (i.e. to the point of not being ill). Then the psychologist would rub his/her hands with glee and move on to the next person who needed 'fixing'.

Except, you see, the job's only half done. Minus 9 to zero is progress, but it's hardly what we would call 'flourishing'. I'm a student of the relatively new field of 'positive psychology', which is about the other end of the spectrum. It's about moving people from, say, a 2 or 3 towards the 7, 8, 9 end of the wellbeing spectrum. There's a massive difference between 'being alive' and 'living'. If you're clever enough to understand the difference then you'll love this section!

Dear God

So far today, I've done alright.

I haven't gossiped. I haven't lost my temper.

I haven't been greedy, moody, nasty or selfish.

And I'm really glad about that.

But in a few minutes, God, I'm going to get out of bed.

And from then on I'm going to need a lot more help.

Thank you.

Amen

From *'Success Intelligence'* by Robert Holden

Chris and Gary asked me to contribute to this book, largely because of my expertise in this area. I have been a student of positive psychology since its inception in 2002. To put it simply, I have been researching happy people! That means finding them (not always easy, remember this is UK research) and seeking out the reasons why they're happier and more positive than the norm.

Just to clarify, I'm not talking about leaping around like Tigger or sticking an inane grin on your face and pretending you're happy. I'm talking about learning some key (very simple) principles that will help you maintain a positive outlook even when the going gets tough. And, as a teacher, it most certainly will! Being upbeat and positive doesn't make Ofsted disappear and it doesn't mean that Connor the 'Lost Boy' from Year 10 is going to behave any better. It simply allows you to be in a better frame of mind to enable you to deal with Ofsted and Connor. I always tell conference audiences that positive psychology doesn't change anything out there, it changes you, in here (please picture me jabbing a finger at my head).

Eeyore walked all round Tigger one way, and then turned and walked round him the other way.

'What did you say it was?' he asked.

'Tigger.'

'Ah!' said Eeyore.

'He's just come,' explained Piglet.

'Ah!' said Eeyore again.

He thought for a long time and then said: 'When is he going?'

A. A. Milne

Dr Feelgood[13]

If you plot people's wellbeing on a graph, you get a rather depressing low level of happiness and

---

[13] No, I'm not talking about the first band Gary saw live!

wellbeing. I won't marinate you in data. Suffice to say, most people are a zillion miles away from feeling as great as they could. And we can get stuck in this curse of mediocrity. The alarm goes off at stupid o'clock in the morning and you have a moment where you think you can't go on. I'm not talking suicide, just an undercurrent of, 'I can't do this any more'. But, of course, you have a mortgage. And responsibilities. So you get on with it, forcing yourself into a routine where you live for the weekend and holidays (remember 'destination addiction' earlier?). Days, weeks and years zip by in a blur and, unknowingly, you get stuck in whinge mode. 'The kids, the parents, the government, the marking, the weather, class 4M...'.

Some people can become seriously entrenched in this default negativity. I call them 'mood hoovers' and, as Gary and Chris have already described, they lurk in the staffroom, waiting to suck every last drop of positivity out of you. It doesn't take many mood hoovers to suck the life out of the school. And, between you, me and the gatepost, if it's the headteacher who's the mood hoover then, Houston, we have a problem![14]

We believe that super-teachers inhabit the other end of the wellbeing spectrum. There are a few people (statistically about 2%) who live much closer to the upper reaches of their range of positivity and happiness. You can spot them a mile off. They smile more. They have energy and a spring in their step. They are solution focused. They have an infectious enthusiasm. The bottom line is that they're happier

---

[14] Classic mood hoover scene from Annie Hall: 'The food here is terrible.' 'Yes, and in such small portions!'

and, get this, other people catch the feeling. So who the hell are these 2%ers? And, more pertinently, what on earth do they do that makes them so happy? And, the million-dollar question... how can we learn to do what they're doing? How can we learn to be happier and more positive?

Good news and bad news. First, the bad. Some people are born with a natural predisposition that will make them miserable (technically, it's called a 'pre-frontal tilt') and it results in chemical imbalances that make you more likely to suffer from depression.

But, good news, almost everyone can learn to be a 2%er. That's so brilliant I'll write it again, but in an even simpler way: **positivity is a learned behaviour!**

My belief is that, as a teaching professional, being happy is the most important thing you will ever learn to do. If you'll allow me to go a step further (the really bright ones among you will already have twigged this bit), there is something called the 'heliotropic effect' whereby plants follow the light. Flowers literally adjust their petals throughout the day to track the sun. And this is where positive psychology, leadership, biology, emotional intelligence, sociology and the law of attraction come together in one big scientific BANG. Please read the next sentence carefully as it has knee-shakingly exciting connotations:

Position yourself in that 2% zone and you give life to others!

Following the light

> *Fear less, hope more; eat less, chew more; whine less, breathe more; talk less, say more; hate less, love more; and good things will be yours.*
>
> **Swedish Proverb**

The heliotropic effect states that all living things are attracted to that which is life giving and repelled by what is life taking. Quite simply, the 2%ers are life-givers. Have you noticed that when you feel great, people around you catch the energy, the confidence, the positivity... whatever it is you're radiating.

Of course, the opposite is also true. That's why mood hoovers suck the energy out of you. Picture the scene; you arrive at a staff meeting full of enthusiasm but the mood hoovers take over. They start with some tutting at agenda item number 1, followed by a sigh and rolling of eyes at 2. It's a blank 'that'll never work' to point 3 and, by then, it's all over. Everyone is low. The spark is extinguished and the seconds tick by on an hour of your life that you're never going to get back. The truth is that as a teacher you've experienced it. The even scarier truth is that you've also inadvertently contributed to it on occasions!

My basic point is that life's a short and precious gift. It's too valuable for you to spend it in the mood hoover zone. Being a 2%er will benefit you, your colleagues and your pupils. And, once you feel great, your behaviours and outcomes will also be upwardly mobile. So, I guess the next question is what on earth do you have to do to become a 2%er?

Read on. Please, read on!

Top tips

1. Don't let the mood hoovers drag you down. Be resilient. Make it your life's work to drag them up!

2. Learn to be positive. Practice hard.

3. Be a 2%er. Give life to others.

Bonus story

ANTs in your PANTs?

We hope not! If you do find a few then my advice is to have a good scratch and, if that doesn't work, change your underwear.

This story isn't about ants in your pants. It's about ANTs in your head. ANTs, you see, are 'automatic negative thoughts'. And we all have them. The damned things convince us we're rubbish, or thick, or that we can't do something. Or that Year 7s only play up for you and that Damien the hell-boy from Year 10 sits like an angel for all the other teachers. ANT's default position is 'can't do', and we're infested.

It's hard to tell what's going on in another person's head. But, a really good mate of mine whom I consider to be a total genius, a brilliant mind and an exceptional human being is, I fear, riddled with automatic negative thoughts. And, despite being a scholar of all things positive, I struggle to find a solution. Because they're his ANTs, not mine. He owns them. He's allowed them to move into his headspace and take over. I can take on the role of the anteater by sticking my long nose into his business and telling him that he's a brilliant man, a total genius and one of the most absurdly awesome human beings I've ever encountered. But his ANTs don't allow him to hear or believe.

He's so clever you see. He's read all the books and been on all the courses. He knows what he needs to do, but he's not doing it. Maybe he likes his ANTs? Maybe they're so familiar that he's got to know them on first name terms? Maybe it's safer to have them aboard? Or easier?

Anyway. I've decided to invent the antidote to ANTs. I call them PANTs - 'positive and nice thoughts'! And if he simply replaced his ANTs with a clean set of PANTs then, hey presto, it's the mental equivalent of Rentokill.

Could be a lesson in there for us all?

Happy PANTs everyone.

Chapter 5

Being brilliant

You're happiest while you're making the greatest contribution.

Robert F. Kennedy

In a nutshell

Hands up if you want to be happier? Thought so! So, here's a question for you; 'Could you be happier even if nothing in the world around you changed?' Got you again!

This section looks at the habits of happy people, distilled into six blindingly obvious points. We examine the 'Law of Attraction' ('I will own that Ferrari, I will own that Ferrari, I will...') and Andy tells his favourite Ofsted story. We conclude with a bit of SUMO, a few HUGGs and a fab bonus story about Monsters Inc. This chapter is the epitome of 'sublime' and 'ridiculous'.

The previous chapter introduced the notion of positive psychology, a newish[15] strand of the subject

---

[15] I say 'newish' to deliberately fudge the issue. Philosophising about 'happiness' has been around pretty much as long as people have, but it's generally acknowledged that 'positive psychology' was 'invented' by Martin Seligman in the early 1990s. Once again 'invented' might be the wrong word. This was the first attempt to bring wellbeing, flourishing, happiness and the science of signature strengths under one academic umbrella.

that takes a look at people who have a feel-good factor and asks three main questions:

1. Who on earth are these people?

2. What are they doing that allows them to be happier and more upbeat than the rest of society?

3. And, crucially, what can we learn from them that we can put into practice in our own lives?

There's plenty of great news folks. Not least the fact that these 'happy people' are normal, just like the rest of us![16] They don't drive Ferraris and they haven't won the lottery. They have the same jobs, weather, mortgage commitments and work pressures as everyone else. You probably know a few. These are colleagues who tussle with the Year 9 hoodlums but, more often than not, seem to come out on top. These are the teachers with verve. They grin a lot and banter with the kids. They radiate energy.

If you were to study these people[17] you'd discover that they have a few positive mental habits (strategies?) that, although they seem to be common sense, are by no means common practice. And, the best news of all, these strategies are very simple and incredibly easy to learn. Now, without wanting to sound mercenary, this is all explained in my book *The Art of Being Brilliant*.

Pour yourself a drink and prepare yourself for the science of the bleedin' obvious. Here is a summary of my six main points, each with a teacher's spin:

---

[16] I use the term 'normal' in its loosest sense of the word!

[17] No need to, I already have!

1. Choose to be positive

Yes, it's that bloomin' simple.[18] The 2%ers consciously and deliberately choose to have a positive approach to life. They go about their daily rounds with a glass-half-full approach to life. Choosing to be positive isn't always easy or obvious, but once you've mastered it, it has genuinely life-giving powers to you and those around you. I'm not talking about a ridiculous happy-clappy-rose-tinted-Pollyanna approach ('Ooooh, we've just failed Ofsted... how super!'), more a positive and realistic approach to life. That means meetings are focused on what you want rather than what you don't want (e.g. a staff meeting about how we're going to wow the inspectors rather than a defensive agenda about how we can hide the bad stuff).

The Law of Attraction

> *You don't fatten a pig by weighing it.*
>
> **Anonymous**

Here's an example. I once did a talk at a school that had failed Ofsted and was due to be re-inspected in a couple of weeks. It was make-or-break time and they were all rather down. I walked into the hall where 80 teachers sat, sapped of energy, some twitching, all with cold sores. If you've ever seen *Shaun of the Dead* you'll know what I mean. In all my years of delivering training I've never seen such a bunch of depressed and exhausted people. You don't need to know much about psychology to know that sitting, rocking

---

[18] Simple but not easy. There is a subtle difference.

yourself in your chair, isn't good (especially if you're the headteacher!). I started with what was, on reflection, not the best line. 'Crikey folks, you look awful!'

'Of course we look awful,' snarled the deputy head, his eye twitching. 'It's Ofsted. They've made us this way.'

'Why?' I inquired. 'What on earth have they done to you?'

'They inspected us!' said another teacher through a cold-sore infested mouth. 'The bastards!'

I think I must have looked slightly perplexed. 'I think that's what they do,' I offered, perhaps less sympathetically than I could have.

'Yes,' hissed the head of maths, 'but they caught us off guard you see. They inspected us in July, when we were on the wind-down to summer. No notice or anything.' She made it sound like something from Die Hard. 'Came in a van. Took over the staffroom. And came round to inspect our classes with their poxy tick sheets.'

'And what did they find?' (Imagine a sympathetic and soothing voice. Like you would use if a pack of Dobermans was circling you.)

'Said we were rubbish teachers. And the kids don't like us. Nor the parents.'

'And we were dead unlucky 'cos it was raining,' interjected a rather drawn woman with sunken eyes.

Again, I shrugged. 'Raining?'

'Yes, you see, the portacabin where Year 7s live has got a hole in the ceiling. And when it rains we have to give the corner table umbrellas. If it hadn't been raining the inspector would never have noticed the hole in the roof. Talk about unlucky!'

(Just so you understand, this is a school in the Midlands. I am not talking about some developing country.) 'Why didn't you fix the hole?' I asked, genuinely puzzled.

'It's only a temporary classroom,' explained the head, rocking gently and staring nowhere in particular.

'Temporary?' I asked. 'How long's it been there?'

'Eighteen years...' came the distant reply.

'And they said the library books were out of date and the computers were old and the printer had run out of ink...'

The maths lady interrupted, close to tears. 'And they're coming back,' she whimpered, her voice trailing off, 'next week.'

Some of the teachers had risen from their seats and were coming at me, zombie like... I calmed them down and coaxed them back to their chairs.

'A question for you guys.' Sunken and bleary eyes turned to me, pleading for answers rather than questions. 'How much is a problem a problem when you're not thinking about it?'

It took a while and there was a murmuring around the room. Eventually the maths lady ventured, 'Well, if you're not thinking about it, it's not a problem.'

There was a gentle murmuring of about 70% agreement. The other 30% were still trying to work out the question.

'So, how much do you think about Ofsted?' I asked.

'All the time,' boomed the head, leaping from his stupor and punching the air in anger. 'Morning, noon and night. I haven't slept for six weeks!'

And herein lay their problem. They were focusing on Ofsted as the enemy. Positive psychology doesn't advocate that you pretend Ofsted will go away, it merely shifts your focus and, as a consequence, makes you more resourceful. Instead of doom and gloom and helplessness, a 2%er would think about what they can do, what outcome they want and, crucially, what steps they have to take to make it happen. Thinking like a 2%er therefore makes you feel more positive about finding a way forward. You fix the roof, change the printer cartridge, restock the library books and prepare some fab lessons. All quick wins. Your energy is restored and Ofsted will sniff the positivity the moment they step through the door.

2. Understand your impact

The second point from my research is about influence and impact. In many ways this is the biggest point for a professional teacher and one that is often forgotten along the way. A quick reminder - human beings are entirely driven by emotions. So, for example, if you buy a new pair of jeans I would argue that you don't really want the jeans, you want the feeling they give you when you pull them on and manage to do the top button up! And that new car... it's not the car that gives you the pleasure, rather the feeling of driving it. If we can get our feelings right, then everything else will follow.

At its most basic level, a human being operates on a 'trigger - feeling - behaviour - outcome' basis. A **trigger** is something out there in the big wide world that makes you **feel** in a certain way. Your feelings drive your **behaviour** which, in turn, determines what happens to you (your **outcome**). For example, the weather is a big trigger. Yet another rainy day can make you feel dismal so you are low on energy and the outcome is that you have an average day. Or, a classic example from my life, someone cutting me up in the traffic! That would automatically make me feel angry. So my behaviour would become aggressive (if you passed through Derby between 1985 and 2005, I apologise. Yes, it was me chasing you across town.) So, there are a million things triggering how you feel every day. What teachers need to understand in the 'trigger - feeling - behaviour -

outcome' model is that you are a trigger! The way you walk into a classroom. What you say and how you say it as you enter the staffroom. The way you contribute (or don't?) in meetings. What you say and how you say it as you get home in the evening. In all of these situations, you are a trigger. You are influencing other people's feelings (which will drive their behaviours and outcomes). The influence you have is huge. The 2%ers understand this and say to themselves, 'if I'm going to have an impact anyway, I may as well strive to make it a positive one.' Hence their predication of positive behaviours.

Applying this to the classroom, think about what you wear. How do you stand? And sit? What kind of words do you use and what tone of voice? If you can come across as positive about yourself, your subject and, more importantly, the children, then you will become the sunshine. You will radiate positivity! The children will become the heliotropes, soaking up the energy and inspiration.

This point is dealt with in some detail in later chapters when we examine specific classroom tactics that will enhance the positive feelings of your 'customers'.

3. Take personal responsibility

Simple so far? I think so. As is the third point, 'personal responsibility'. Briefly, the transition from 'mood hoover' to '2%er' doesn't happen by accident. It requires effort. In fact, in my case, it required a considerable degree of personal change and the bottom line is that nobody's going to do it for you. You don't just wake up one day magically transformed into a positive, effervescent, enthusiastic teacher. How many people do you know who are moaning and groaning about their lot but when you examine their life, they're moaning about the same stuff they moaned about five years ago? And nothing's changed! The 2%ers don't point the finger at everyone else, blaming the head or Ofsted or the parents or kids. The super-teacher will point the finger back at themselves and ask, 'What can I do differently to get a better result?' Or basically, 'How can I change me?'

Please note, pointing the finger back at yourself is not blaming yourself, it's empowering yourself. Blame leaves you lethargic and paralysed; empowerment gives you energy and resourcefulness.

I once heard it thus: do you want results or excuses? I know an awful lot of people who are on the excuses end of life. Super-teachers are wary of those who ratchet up the 'excuse machine' as to why the kids won't learn anything in a particular lesson. Have you ever heard any of these?

'It's Monday morning, they are half asleep!'

'It's Friday afternoon. They never settle on Friday afternoon!'

'It's hot!'[19]

'It's too hard for these kids.'

'It's Sports' Day/School photographs/the School Nurse's visit... they'll be over excited!'

Super-teachers place themselves firmly at the 'results' end of the equation. 'What am I going to do to make it happen?'

---

[19] You can substitute 'windy', 'rainy' or 'foggy'. We grudgingly accept that 'snowy' is a genuine one because we want to go and throw snowballs too!

Incidentally, teenagers find this the hardest of the points to action. I've lost track of the number of times I've spoken to the low achievers and asked them why they're failing at school. 'It's the teachers' fault sir, they're rubbish.' Or, the classic, 'lessons are too boring'. I'm fascinated by this shift of responsibility from oneself to other people and I believe personal responsibility comes with maturity. The sooner we twig that (excuse the cliché) life's not a rehearsal, the sooner we start to make positive things happen in our lives.

4. Bouncebackability or resilience

Bouncebackability (yes, it's in the dictionary) is a toughie. Positive psychology doesn't say that you can live happily and positively forever and ever, Amen. Quite the contrary. There are times when life will be awful. The death of a loved one, redundancy, marriage break-up, serious illness - all of these are legitimate reasons to feel terrible. In a teaching context, a truly awful lesson, a bad inspection report, a horrible parent - all legitimate reasons for feeling low. And, inevitably, 2%ers do sometimes feel terrible! But they have a high degree of bouncebackability (or, if you prefer something that sounds a little more scientific, resilience), enabling them to spring back to being upbeat and happy. This is tied in closely with 'choose to be positive' because if you are a genuinely upbeat person you have a better chance of bouncing back from adversity. But, I guess this is good news for us all folks, you are allowed to have a bad lesson, awful day or terrible week. Just not a terrible life!

There's a great book called SUMO by Paul McGee. In it he talks of 'hippo time', when you can legitimately wallow in whatever it is you want to wallow in. But get the wallowing out of your system before you drag everyone else into the mire! Paul McGee lists these great questions as a way of helping you gain some perspective and energy to move forward:

1. Where is this issue on a scale of 1 to 10?

2. How important will this be in twelve months' time?

3. Is my response appropriate and effective?

4. How can I influence or improve the situation?

5. What can I learn from this?

6. What will I do differently next time?

7. What can I find that's positive in this situation?

5. HUGGs

Everyone needs a HUGG, right? 'Huge unbelievably great goals' are another feature of positive people. While most teachers' goal is simply to 'get through the day' a super-teacher has bigger aims. A HUGG is a twelve to twenty-four-month whopper of a goal. To get promoted, to get a headship, to gain the best results in the school, county or country! These truly inspirational goals sit at the edges of your achievability and are only possible if you have a genuinely positive approach. The truth is that most people drift through life, their weeks and months zipping by in a blur. A HUGG gives you focus, drive and direction.

Mr Best believed in setting his pupils big goals.

In terms of implementing this within the classroom I rather like Ben Zander's activity in *The Art of Possibility*. At the start of the year he asks his students to write him a letter entitled, 'I got my grade A because...'. This is a great way of getting learners to consider, at the outset, the kinds of attitudes and behaviours that will make them successful.

6. Play to your strengths

And our final habit of positivity is to play to your strengths. Once again, it seems intuitively obvious - you will feel and perform better if you're allowed to do what you do best - yet many organisations are set up to the contrary. Organisations spend a great deal of time recruiting people with the right skills for the job and then spend the next ten years trying to plug their weaknesses! It happened to me when I worked in the corporate world. I was recruited as a trainer presumably because I had the right skill set they were looking for. Great stuff. And then they realised I was rubbish at spreadsheets so sent me on an Excel course! On reflection, their time, money and my effort would have been much better spent on training me in something I was already great at. That way, I'd have achieved giant leaps of learning. So, if you're a creative person you'll feel invigorated when you're allowed to be creative. If you're artistic, then find a way of working art into your repertoire.

Our advice is two-fold. First, be aware of what your strengths are. This sounds obvious but I'm always astounded that people have very little awareness of what their signature strengths are.[20]

Second, be aware of your weaknesses and plug them if they're causing you to be incompetent or unsafe, but don't spend your career worrying about what you're rubbish at. It saps your energy. Everyone has weaknesses. Chill. Focus on working to your strengths and, where possible, invest in making your strengths stronger.

By choosing a positive approach to your job, not only will it help you enjoy it more but it will have side effects. Your positivity will rub off on others. Your peers and your pupils will feed from your positivity. You will be noted for your positive approach which may well open up opportunities for you, possibly promotion. At the very least you will be highly valued

---

[20] People are much more forthcoming if I ask them about their weaknesses!

by the school's leaders.[21] Learning in your lessons will be more enjoyable and fun. And remember what we have said about making learning fun. You will leave work each day feeling good and the next day will never feel like it is a chore. Consequently you will get up for work looking forward to it.

You could be in the career for 30+ years so it helps to feel good about it!

Top tips

1. Never ever become a 'mood hoover'. In every school there will be at least one. Watch and listen closely. Learn how not to be one!

2. Practise the six points of being a 2%er. Go out of your way to make someone's day. Practise being upbeat until it becomes your default setting.

3. Appreciate that you are allowed to have a bad day. But learn to bounce back into the positive zone rather than spending excessive time wallowing.

Bonus story

Monsters Inc.

If you've seen Monsters Inc. you'll know it's a cool movie. If you haven't seen it... what are you waiting for?

Sully is a blue, hairy, hulk of a monster. His buddy, Mike, is well... an eye. On legs. And they are a team. They work for 'Monsters Incorporated', a

---

[21] Important point to note, those teachers held in highest regard in senior leadership meetings are invariably those who have a positive attitude. Infectious enthusiasm and a 'can do' attitude will get you noticed for all the right reasons.

huge organisation that employs monsters to scare children into screaming. They then bottle the screams to create electricity that powers their city (Monstropolis, where else!)

The children are scared of the monsters and, interestingly, the monsters have been taught to be scared of the children. With me so far?

Except Sully messes up big time. The big blue buffoon accidentally brings a child back to Monstropolis. And he finds that the child (Boo) is a sweet, innocent thing. And Boo has no fear of Sully. I guess she's not learned to be scared. The breakthrough comes when Mike and Sully discover that Boo's laughter also creates power. And then it's a good old-fashioned battle between the old way (creating fear) versus the new way (creating happiness).

It's such a great idea for a movie. And the clincher is when they discover that laughter has ten times more power than fear. Imagine! So the monsters have to change their approach, adopting silly hats and churning out smiles instead of roars. It seems the new way is more powerful than the old.

Part 2

The art of teaching

At last, the supposed 'book about teaching' actually gets around to some teaching. About time! Except we don't, at least not straight away. This part starts with a look at the planning stage. We state a lot more bleedin' obvious stuff about the importance of being organised and creating a learning environment where pupils feel at their best. We discuss the need to plan 'awe' and 'wonder' into your lessons. Then we look at how to kick off a lesson, how to create engagement and how to finish with a flourish.

6. **Planning 1: Selling your message**

7. **Planning 2: The learning environment**

8. **Teaching 1: The perfect start**

9. **Teaching 2: Engagement**

10. **Teaching 3: The grand finale**

Chapter 6

Planning 1:
Selling your message

A little less conversation, a little more action please.

Elvis Presley

In a nutshell

At last, we get around to the 'how to teach' bit. Or do we? Brace yourself for some information about the human race and some bleedin' obvious advice on planning and being organised. Not sexy, but spot on! The chapter starts with a reflective exercise, before exploding with some calorific stories involving Maltesers and Cadbury's Creme Eggs! We look briefly at the 7 Ps and how to write learning aims. We d-d-deal with decibels, differentiation and dyslexia, before finishing with how to teach key words and plan for pupils who have ants in their pants (whom the establishment calls 'kinaesthetic learners'). In essence, this chapter is about planning to bring life into your lessons. We throw in a bit of Sinatra and finish with a rather clever piece about an animal school.

Pause for thought

Grab a glass of Iron-Bru[22] or whatever takes your fancy and spend a bit of time thinking about these questions. Relax and reflect on what you've read so far and connect with your past.

1. Who was the best teacher you had at school?

2. Think about what made them so special.

3. Were they special to others too?

4. How did they make you feel?

5. How hard did you work for them?

6. What's the learning from this activity?

Now that you've remembered Mr Snidgepodge and how he used to make the whole class laugh by putting on the voices of characters in the novels you read, how can you have that sort of impact on your pupils?

The human race

Picture the scene...

You are looking down on a maternity ward, a silent witness to the miracle of new life arriving on earth. The mother-to-be is sucking deeply on gas and air and gripping her partner's hand so tight it has lost all feeling. The midwife is taking care of the business end of proceedings and at regular intervals issuing the instruction, 'push at the next contraction'. Amid this cacophony of sucking, grimacing, squeezing and pushing noises, a baby is born - a boy. The

---

[22] Other fizzy drinks are available.

midwife takes the baby in her arms and quickly but carefully raises him to lie on the heaving chest of his mother, saying, 'It's a boy Mrs Charlton, looks like he'll be crap at maths like you were, but you know, I think he's going to be gifted at football.'

The proud father looks up and, with a wry smile, adds, 'I was crap at maths as well... and English.'

Now I'm not Hercule Poirot, but I think there's something fishy going on here. Do we as teachers really believe kids are born with predestined talents? Do we actually think that gifted anthropologists pop out of the womb ready to get stuck into ancient history? Or architects are born with grand designs already in their heads? Surely not, yet throughout my career I have heard teacher after teacher talk about 'talented kids' and 'less able kids' as if that is how they were designed and would be forever.

Just today I was visiting a primary school and the headteacher showed me the exercise book of a Year 3 pupil. The work was beautifully written, in a handwriting style of a teenager, with words correctly spelled and used in simple and complex sentences.

Had I just witnessed the work of a child prodigy, a child so naturally gifted that by the age of seven she is writing like a fifteen year old? A child in the mould of Dickens? A genius?

Not at all! Dickens may well have been pretty good at writing when he was a lad. And Mozart may well have been a wonderful pianist at the age of six, but by that time his father, a composer and high-quality musician in his own right, had provided his son with around 3,500 hours of quality practice. The same is true of our young writer. From an early age her parents had read to her, encouraged her to use a pen to form the words they enjoyed together and instilled in her a love for the written word. They began the process of teaching her to write as soon as she could hold a pen.

So not 'gifted or talented' at all, just given a head start in the human race!

This explains why Gary has never played football for Newcastle United! Alas, his boyhood dream was never to be fulfilled. Despite the fact that he loved playing football, there was no quality coaching at any of the schools he attended and no youth team in the small village he grew up in. However, he was good at art at school, and this was because he was copying his mother, an amateur artist, from an early age. By 6 he'd already used oil paints.[23] There might have been a bit of art in his DNA but it still needed recognising and nurturing.

So what we want you to understand is that all kids have the potential for greatness.[24] Continuing the 'human race' analogy, our job as teachers is to play catch-up as fast as possible with those who lag behind, while also stretching those who are past the first bend.

Let's look at the slow starters. We are constantly in the business of dealing with a deficit start at school.

---

[23] The illustrations in this book are the work of Gary Toward, age fifty-one and three-quarters.

[24] I once worked with some Year 11s who had been written off by the education system. It turned out that one of them could break into a Mercedes CLS (a notoriously 'hard-to-break-into vehicle' in the car crime world) in under ten seconds. Gifted and talented in the extreme, just not channelled in the right direction!

Many kids will arrive at their first reception class with an academic self-concept already established due to the subliminal and overt messages they pick up at home. Mum, dad (or whoever) has never read them a bedtime story. They've never been encouraged to write or draw. They've never had praise or boundaries.

Back to the self-fulfilling prophecy at the birth scene earlier. You just know our newborn baby is not going to be good at maths and English, don't you?

Now, you might be thinking that your job is to teach science or food technology. That's what they said in the interview, right? Or maybe you major in PE with a bit of history thrown in? Or you teach Key Stage 1, in which case your job can be narrowed down to getting the kids to grasp the basics of literacy and numeracy. Right?

Err... 100% wrong! We think it's your job to unpick those limiting beliefs. We're not saying it's easy, especially if you're fighting against a home culture of apathy, but we're suggesting it's your duty. And this is where super-teachers have the edge. They don't just deliver curriculum, they deliver inspiration, self-belief and unbridled enthusiasm for human potential. And they don't just retain their enthusiasm for two or three years. It's a bit like a puppy, folks. This is for life!

At the same time, you can't just expect those who are intrinsically motivated and already boosted in their learning to just keep striding ahead. Let's think back to Mozart. Did he just develop naturally beyond his sixth birthday to compose some of the most incredible music ever written, or was he continually challenged by his father to gradually increase his ability? Young Mozart[25] was stretched. His potential was recognised, nurtured and given a chance to develop into something extraordinary. So, while not everyone in your classroom is going to be a child prodigy, we believe that super-teachers will bring out the best in each and every pupil, no matter where they line up in the human race.

The 7 Ps

There are very few teachers who can wing it. Those that do are either very good, very lucky or don't care about the quality of the learning.[26] While 'thinking on your feet' is a crucial quality for super-teachers, our message is that if you consistently 'wing it', you will get found out.

> *It's only when the tide goes out that you learn who's been swimming naked.*
>
> **Warren Buffett**

You might have heard of the 7 Ps?[27] It's not a very glamorous message folks, but a great lesson usually comes from effort you put in at the planning stage.

When it comes to putting a lesson together, I find I go through much the same process whether it is a lesson, an assembly, an after-dinner speech or a training session. I start by thinking, 'What is the main objective?' and then, 'How am I going to sell this to my audience? How will I get them on board?'

---

[25] 'Wolfie', as he was known to his mates in the playground.

[26] These kind of teachers are unlikely to ever pick up this book

[27] Prior planning and preparation prevents p*** poor performance.

In a wider context, creativity, innovation and engagement are the keys to raising educational achievement. It doesn't take lashings of money, it doesn't require flashy new school buildings and it doesn't need a different school system. It simply takes brilliantly creative teaching, which logically flows from planning.

Many of the techniques in this chapter can be found in any teacher training handbook. Where *The Art of Being a Brilliant Teacher* is different is in this crucial area of 'How am I going to sell this?' Any teacher worth their salt is going to sit down and think, 'What are the children going to learn in this lesson?' but super-teachers then decide how they are going to get their kids interested. What is the hook? What is it that is going to make their pupils sit up and take notice? Remember, there is often no obvious reason as to why kids should want to learn whatever you have in store for them. You have got to engage them in wanting to learn! And, to be honest, this is often the hardest part of teaching. How do I make quadratic equations interesting? How can I inspire Year 4s to learn their times tables? How can I engage teenagers in King Lear? How on earth am I going to get Year 9 boys interested in making pastry? Or, possibly the most daunting of all, how am I going to grab and hold the attention of the whole school in assembly?

There are a lot of magic ingredients but a key one is... *imagination!*

Imagination is more important than knowledge.

Albert Einstein

Let me give you an example. I recently watched a PE lesson in which the teacher was teaching how to run a relay race. In the previous lesson, despite extensive practice, the kids kept dropping the baton. At the beginning of the next lesson, she produced a large tube of Maltesers. Cue great excitement. 'If we make it round the track without dropping it, we share the Maltesers.' Not one child dropped the baton in that lesson, and when she went on next lesson to producing the original baton, their skills had noticeably improved![28] The Maltesers didn't just magically turn up in that lesson. This teacher had used imagination at the planning stage.

A business studies teacher was making the rather tricky point of 'diminishing marginal utility' to some hard-core Year 11s who, quite frankly, didn't want to be there. She produced five Creme Eggs and asked for a volunteer. Thirty hands shot up! The volunteer's challenge was simply to eat the eggs and record their satisfaction on a scale of 1 to 10. Egg number 1 was scoffed with gusto and rated a 10. Egg number 2 was eaten with almost equal vigour and given a 9. Egg 3 was accompanied by, 'I feel a bit sick miss' and a score of 4. Egg 4 was forced down (and nearly returned) and the teenager staggered to the board to record a meek score of 1. Egg 5 remained unopened. Now, while I'm not necessarily recommending you do this activity, the pupil had demonstrated the law of diminishing marginal utility and the learners will probably remember that class forever. Once again, engagement was planned in way before the lesson was delivered.

---

[28] And they went on to win the inter-school relay event!

And it doesn't have to revolve exclusively around sweets and chocolate! A difficult Year 9 text set in the French Revolution contained the phrase, *elle va épouser son petit ami*. None of the kids knew the word *épouser*, until, that is, the teacher hit them with the Wedding March at full volume, accompanied by confetti. Unforgettable for the kids, and well worth the clearing up afterwards!

We are what we repeatedly do. Excellence, therefore, is not an act but a habit.

Aristotle

This is where super-teachers are different. One of the criticisms that most children (and parents) have is that some subjects don't seem relevant. Find the relevance and you become the sort of teacher who these kids will remember for the rest of their lives. The subject comes to life and it means that you will have enjoyable and rewarding lessons rather than simply trying to keep on top of them. An ex-colleague would typically reply, when asked the question, 'How was your lesson today?' by saying, 'They weren't too bad...'. The assumption was that the kids would be uninterested and inattentive. Super-teachers look forward to every lesson because they have the chance to weave their magic spell of engagement.

Food for thought

A child of five would understand this. Send someone to fetch a child of five!

Grouch Marx

First things first; you need to decide what the pupils are going to learn. Then start to chunk the lesson into at least three parts. How will the lesson start, from the moment they come through the door? What will happen then? What is the main learning activity? How will the lesson end? Think of the lesson as a three-course meal: starter, main course, pud. Of course, this basic model can be refined according to your exact circumstances, but it gives you a basic structure. You need to be very clear about what the learning is to be and be very sure it is the right learning pitched at the right levels for the individuals in the class. It is important that you grasp the idea that a learning aim is not a doing aim. This is the difference between lessons that turn out well by design or succeed or fail by accident. Let's just return to the basics again. Lessons are about learning.

Here's an example of how you can get it wrong or right:

✗ The learning aim is to write some similes and metaphors.

✓ The learning aim is for the pupils to be able to understand the difference between similes and metaphors and how they can be used in descriptive writing.

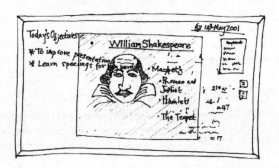

We don't want to be pedantic but this *really* matters. If you do not know what the learning is to be, *exactly*, then how can you expect your pupils to?

Always bear in mind pupils' likely attention span. Those who have researched these learned matters have concluded that the average attention span for an adult is about twelve minutes. And you are teaching children! If you are expecting them to listen for any more than that, you are being over-optimistic.

Decibels

We now come to a major decision area - working noise! This is one area where super-teachers are quite different from the rest. I have seen more lessons create less learning than they could have done because of this than for any other single reason. Let us start by reminding ourselves what we know about learning styles. We know that some people are *interpersonal* learners, while others are *intrapersonal* learners. In other words, some people learn by talking and working with others, while others need quiet so that they can concentrate and figure it out.

You need to create the sort of environment that accommodates both types of learners, giving those who learn by talking opportunities to do so in the lesson's learning tasks, but when you want solo work, insist on it. Even the interpersonal learners need to learn to be self-sufficient and, of course, it lets the intrapersonal learners enter their secure learning zone.

There are stages in your lesson when you are going to want group discussion and activity, but there will also be parts of your lesson that will be far more effective if pupils are working in silence. I watched a science lesson recently that contained a good blend of activities in the first half, which were well focused on the learning aims. The moment then came when the pupils had to write up their findings in their books. There was idle chatter going on all around the classroom and very little learning. At that point they should have been whipped into order and made to do the written work in silence. They would have completed the work much more quickly and they would have grasped the concepts much more effectively. Super-teachers create the right environment for effective learning and sometimes, that means, silence.

There are other considerations to bear in mind as well. Think of what time of day the lesson is to take place. Secondary teachers often teach the same lesson twice to two parallel groups, but there could be a world of difference between first thing in the morning and last thing in the afternoon. Think of what comes before your lesson. Have the kids been out doing PE and do they always arrive in dribs and drabs, puffing and panting? Are they always high after music or drama? The weather will also have a significant impact. Yes, it really is true! On windy and rainy days pupils will be much more unsettled. Instead of using this as an excuse, you need to develop ways that will invigorate or calm them (as appropriate). Your job is to get them into 'learning mode' as quickly as possible.

Differentiation

What are the other ingredients to put into the mixing bowl to come up with a super-lesson? Differentiation is one of them and it's still one of the hardest nuts to crack when you are teaching day in, day out.

It is hard enough preparing one complete set of wunderlessons, without having to nip and tuck each one to cater for all the different learners in your classroom! In every single class of thirty kids, there will always be those who struggle and those who zip through the work. Of those who finish first, there will be diligent ones who have picked up what to do and executed it to near perfection, and there will be those who have done it slap dash, just to get it done. Proper differentiation is no easy task, but it is something which super-teachers plan into their lessons.

This takes us back to your learning aim. What do you want all of your pupils to learn? What, then, do you want a specific number of others to learn beyond that? And are there any really zippy individuals you can stretch even further?

First let us think of those early finishers. Make it easy on yourself. Whenever possible have something else for them to do. This can be a range of generic tasks, such as 'Think of two questions we do not yet know the answers to relating to what we are learning,' or 'Think of another task we could use to practise what we are learning today' or, my favourite, 'In what other context could we apply what we have learned today?'

Sometimes these old chestnuts can be complemented by another activity which will extend the learning further. Try to avoid simply giving a pupil *more* to do. For example, for the pupil who has just finished doing twenty sums it isn't much of an incentive to be told to do ten more! Try to think of a next stage in the learning. I watched a superb humanities lesson about the *Titanic* recently and, for those who completed quickly the written task that focused on empathy, the teacher had prepared an account of the sinking of the Lusitania. Brilliant! It was interesting and didn't replicate what had already been achieved. The children being challenged were then asked to compare the way the passengers, and then the crew, reacted in the two sinkings, looking for similarities and differences. Some were extended even further by asking why they thought there might have been differences. Very effective and, I have to say, quite simple for the teacher to organise. I might add that those children loved being stretched.

Now let us think about those whose rate of learning may be slower than the main bulk of the class. You will obviously find that they benefit from greater attention from either you or your assistant (if you are lucky enough to have one). It's vital that in your planning you really do communicate well with any classroom assistants to ensure that their differentiation work is precise and targeted. There's nothing worse than seeing a classroom assistant who is simply a security blanket for the teacher and is very much making it up as they go.

The glory of different coloured paper allows you to be very creative with producing worksheets suitably adapted in a way that is easy for you to administer to the right pupils. Think of different ways you can set homework assignments as well. I have seen many a lesson with a nod towards differentiation during the lesson, followed by a homework task that was common to all.

Allow for different learning styles to come into play. If you have pupils who are stronger at drawing and illustrating than writing, explore how you can weave that into the tapestry of their learning.

Recently, I saw a very skilful English teacher working with a challenging class of Year 9s on the topic of First World War poetry, not perhaps natural territory for these kids, but a magic moment was created when the teacher invited one lad, who was known to be heavily into rap, to produce a rap for his homework. This teenager was totally uninterested in homework, and didn't usually bother very much, except insofar as he needed to keep out of detentions. This particular piece of homework was emailed to his teacher next morning and was absolutely brilliant. His learning had deepened through it. It was even more special when he rapped it to the class and impacted on their learning. Differentiation, par excellence!

Dyslexia

I picked up some very useful tips during the recent Dyslexia Week at our school. I well remember one dyslexic child telling me that when he looked at the screen, what he could see resembled a big tangled roll of barbed wire with all the letters jumping around. Imagine that, day after day after day, from the moment you start school! When you present written work, either on the screen or on a worksheet, enlarge the font to 14 or even 16 point size if you can. This will immediately help. Then use different colours for your fonts. A sea of black will be very intimidating and can quickly lead to giving up! Breaking up the text with blues and reds increases accessibility at a stroke. Think also about your background. White is a very harsh and startling background that glares at the kids. A softer pastel colour will help. Finally, break up the text with pictures, illustrations, photographs or cartoons. There are lots of easily downloadable materials on the internet and it will make the world of difference to the readability of what you have put in front of the class. It also serves the purpose of broadcasting on the kids' wavelength. I have seen pretty sterile screen displays suddenly brought to life by the inclusion of a favourite cartoon character or a well-known TV personality.

Key words

You will almost certainly plan that your pupils will learn some key words during your lesson. The most important thing about key words is that if you have got them, use them! I have watched lessons where the teacher has prepared beautiful key words, all nicely laminated and stuck on the board at the front, but they were never used. Having gone to all that trouble, use them! Remember that key words will help your visual learners but will not, on their own, be of any help to children with other learning styles. This didn't occur to me for the first twenty-five years of my teaching career! Because I am a visual learner, I had always assumed that if you wrote a word up, then children would learn it. Not so! You need to make a conscious effort to teach those key words. Plan to get pupils out to move them, rearrange them, order them, share them, talk about them... or use them as a means of teaching literacy, because remember we are all teachers of literacy! Plan to ask the children to tell you which word would come first in the dictionary, which would come last, which order would the others come in? How many syllables are there in each one? Can they think of a word that rhymes with one of the words? Or a word that starts the same way?

How many key words should you have in a lesson? My instinct here is that you should aim for five or six maximum. I think it is very hard to do justice to more than that, and if they are really key words, then they will not fulfil their function if they are simply wallpaper at the front of your room. It is much better to have fewer words and really teach to them. The other consideration is where to put them. Much research suggests that it is far more effective if they are above the kids' eye line. It is much better to have them at the top of your board or your displays, and they will have a much greater impact.

Up and about

Now to kinaesthetic learning. You will almost certainly have been on an accelerated learning course and learned about VAK (visual-auditory-kinaesthetic) learning. In a sense we start to do the full circle here because, if you ask previous generations of students, when you meet them years later, who their favourite teachers were and what it is that they remember, they almost always refer to stunts in class of one sort or another.[29] If you were to track a child through their day, I think you would find that the overwhelming majority of the time they are sitting at a desk, listening, reading or writing. What compounds this situation is that those are precisely the things that a lot of children are not very good at! You will have many kinaesthetic learners in your classrooms, kids who learn by doing things rather than reading and writing them. They need to use their bodies and move around to help them learn. Again, this a key ingredient for super-teachers and kinaesthetic learning needs to be planned in. So here are some examples:

---

[29] The only geography lesson I can clearly recall is the one when Mr Hatcher took us outside on a blazing afternoon because it was too hot and stuffy indoors. 'Tectonic plates' was expertly delivered to thirty excited Year 9s under a willow tree.

- When learning new spellings, get the pupils to spell the words with their fingers in the air, or you can put them in pairs and get them to spell the word on their partner's back so they have to say what the word is.

- Difficult concepts can often be learned easily by getting the kids up and out of their seats. Here's an example that's embedded in most science teachers' repertoire. It is easy for kids to understand what happens to gases, liquids and solids when they are heated by getting the kids to stand up in groups. The gases stand a metre apart, the liquids stand closer together and the solids stand shoulder to shoulder, and then they have to jiggle around. It is fun and illustrates the learning perfectly.

- Sticking with science, in a lesson on the planets the children very quickly learn which order the planets are in if you get them out to the front. The first kid you ask to be the Sun (with lots of wiping of the brow because it is hot!); the second one is Mercury and you get that kid to walk around the Sun to teach what an orbit is; the third one is Venus... and so on. Or take them out onto the playground. Pluto can go and stand at the furthest end of the field to illustrate just how far away it actually is.[30]

- Moving on to English, I watched a very effective lesson on Richard III with a Year 10 group, in which it had become apparent in the previous lesson that they had not grasped why there was such

---

[30] Make sure you keep waving to Pluto. And when he gets back, ask him how it was to be so far away from the Sun. Cue more learning!

controversy about the throne. So the teacher took them back to Edward III. A pupil was invited to come and sit on a chair at the front, holding a card that said Edward III. Another chair was added for Edward's son, the Black Prince, and a third for his son, Richard II. The teacher then told the story of the demise of the Black Prince so that Richard II inherited the throne, but he had no children. More chairs were added to show how the claims to the throne passed down through the Houses of Lancaster and York with the resulting Wars of the Roses. Of course it was all embellished with an assortment of paper crowns and plastic swords which the kids loved. The whole thing took ten minutes and at the end one pupil hung back and thanked the teacher and said, 'I think I've actually understood it now!'

It was a brilliant interactive presentation, the kids loved it and, most importantly, they learned what they needed to know. It was a magic moment and that is what super-teachers do that other teachers don't. The early generation of Ofsted inspectors talked about 'awe and wonder' - those moments that provide memorable learning. Super-teachers conjure up these magic learning experiences which pupils remember forever.

Do it Sinatra's way

These are only examples. Every teacher will work out their own way of creating a magic learning experience. When I was a head of department, colleagues would often say, 'I am not like you! I am not a circus performer!' Happily they are right! They are not like me.[31] So I used to say, 'Fine, that's

---

[31] I wouldn't wish that on anyone!

not a problem. Do it your own way. But don't not do it!' Super-teachers have the kids eating out of their hands because their lessons have that vital ingredient. It doesn't matter how you create it. You must work on what works for you, but it is worth its weight in gold. It gets your kids on board, and then you can teach them something.

Another great source of inspiration could be broadly described as 'amazing facts'. A PE lesson on long jump to a group of testosterone-filled, pubescent boys was turned on its head when the teacher produced a measuring tape which showed the world record for long jump. In fact there was an audible intake of breath from all the boys! I saw a similar thing with a javelin lesson where the teacher had placed a pole in the ground at the world record distance. Jaws dropped.

But, it's important to note that in all of these examples, the teacher planned for 'awe and wonder', build it in as a habit.

Top tips

1. Prepare. Prepare. Prepare.

2. Plan to be imaginative.

3. Have clear learning objectives.

4. Don't stress about 'differentiation'. Make it easy on yourself and the learners by asking 'in what other context can today's learning be applied?'

5. Make your lessons active.

Bonus story

The animal school[32]

Once upon a time the animals decided they must organise themselves to meet the problems of the new world. So they organised a school.

They adopted an activity-based curriculum consisting of the essentials in life, namely running, climbing, swimming and flying. To make it easier to administer the curriculum all the animals took all the subjects.

The duck was excellent at swimming, in fact better than his instructor, but he was only average at flying and was very poor at running. Since he was slow in running he had to stay after school and also drop swimming in order to practise running. This was kept up until his webbed feet were badly worn and he was only average at swimming.

The rabbit started at the top of the class in running but had a nervous breakdown brought on by the pressure of having to learn to swim and fly.

The squirrel was excellent in climbing class. She tried to teach the others but over-exerted herself and ended with a C in climbing and D in running, failing flying and swimming altogether.

The eagle was a problem pupil and was severely disciplined. In the climbing class she beat all the others to the top of the tree but insisted on using her own way of getting there. The teacher was annoyed that she failed to follow the climbing instructions and her wings were clipped as

---

[32] We'll let you work out the moral of this fable.

punishment. Now she couldn't fly at all and was learning to run instead.

At the end of the year an abnormal eel that could swim exceedingly well and also run and fly a little had the highest average and was hailed as 'top of the class'. He died soon after as a result of an unfortunate climbing accident.

The dogs stayed out of school and fought the authorities because they wouldn't add digging and retrieving to the curriculum.

Chapter 7

Planning 2: The learning environment

Piglet lay there, wondering what had happened. At first he thought that the whole world had blown up; and then he thought that perhaps only the forest part of it had; and then he thought that perhaps only he had, and he was now alone in the moon or somewhere, and he would never see Christopher Robin or Pooh or Eeyore again. And then he thought, 'Well, even if I'm in the moon, I needn't be face downwards all the time,' so he got cautiously up and looked about him.'

A. A. Milne

In a nutshell

This chapter starts with that superb Piglet passage above and goes from strength to strength. We point out the value of subconscious learning and suggest that if you take care of the little things, the big stuff is more likely to work out for you. We point out that your learners only really require three things of you. First, that you control them. Second, that they learn something and, third, that they enjoy the learning process. Your lesson starts as they enter the room, so we look at the sights, sounds and smells that greet them. Oh, and there's a laugh-out-loud story about the three bears to finish with. Priceless!

Still at the planning stage, but now to some pith! What are the age-old ingredients of a really good lesson? You know when you have taught a really good lesson, there's a lovely sense of satisfaction deep inside. You can't wait to tell someone else about how brilliant it was. Of course, we are all well brought up and modesty has been drummed into us, but when you have had a real triumph, especially perhaps with a tricky class, it makes you feel so good you want to shout it from the rooftops!

Where does your lesson start?

The answer to that is 'before the first pupils even come near the threshold of your room'. It is our firm belief, based on the experience of having taught and observed thousands of lessons, that it is very hard work rescuing a lesson that has got off to a bad start. This chapter is devoted to the first five minutes of the lesson and is divided into two parts: before the children arrive and once they are all seated and ready to learn.

In all aspects of teaching, getting the little things right means you rarely have large problems. In lesson planning, those little things are crucial and can easily make the difference between a decidedly average lesson and an excellent one. Consider whether children are coming to your class because they have to, or because they want to.

So what do you need to think about before they arrive? Let us start with a reminder of the three fundamental demands that all children make of their teacher.

- First, that the teacher controls them. And, yes, they will make it as difficult as possible for you to do so in the early stages, just to test you out and see if you can really do it!

- Second, that they learn something.

- And, third, that they enjoy the learning process. We appreciate that not every lesson can be an all-singing all-dancing gala performance but, overall, is there an environment in your classroom where enjoyment is actively encouraged?

In terms of an expectation to learn, yes, children are really very old fashioned about this. They expect to learn something from you. It is the only reason you all find yourselves in the same room at the same time! They know and you know and their parents know that school is, first and foremost, a place of learning.

> *A good thing sells itself. A bad one advertises itself.*
>
> **Anonymous**

First things first then - they demand that you control them. I know, I know... if you think of your worst class of the week there will be a voice in your head at this point saying that the last thing they seem to want is to be 'controlled'. Trust me. It's true. I don't necessarily mean 'controlled' in terms of bellowing at them or using a metaphorical big stick. I'm talking about children wanting structure, authority and respect. We're back to the question of earlier - do pupils come to your class because they have to or because they want to? This book is about striving to achieve the latter, which means the first few minutes can be make-or-break.

Subconscious messages

He who laughs, lasts.

Mary Poole

We know from research by people far more intelligent than us who spend hours, days and years studying these things at universities that the overwhelming majority of what we learn, we learn subconsciously.

What are the subconscious messages being sent out by your classroom before the pupils even set foot inside? Please bear in mind that the tiniest details have an impact on how we feel. And you need to design a classroom that feels great. How do the chairs and tables look? Are they arranged in a neat and orderly manner or have they been left anyhow from the previous session? It's your learning environment. Nothing would send me a stronger message that this teacher isn't on top of things and isn't in control than finding chairs and tables in disarray as I walked into the room. It might seem minor, but we believe it's actually a big deal in terms of setting the tone for learning.

You need to plan for a great start. It is well worth your while keeping the pupils at bay for a second or two longer to get the room as you want it and to make sure the computer is ready to roll, rather than scrabbling around trying to get things straight while they are asking you questions and getting themselves settled. Nothing's worse than frantically trying to find the presentation you are after, while some of your most trying pupils arrive and greet you, as they do almost every lesson with, 'Did we have any homework?'

Andy goes a step further. Your classroom looks right, but do you? Before anyone comes into your classroom, smooth yourself down, stand tall, greet them as they come through the door. Be alive. Be smart. Be a model of enthusiasm.

'Morning Martha, thank you for looking so smart.'

'Hi James, take a seat and get ready for a fabulous lesson.'

'Connor, I checked your homework last night and it's the best you've ever done for me. I'm delighted with your effort. Thank you.'

James always had the correct equipment for Mr Garlic's lesson.

Now, temperature and smells. Yes, indeed! When you are working in a room all day, you become almost immune to the prevailing ambience of the room. Remember our assertion that it makes your task doubly difficult if you have to rescue a bad start. What can be worse than when each succeeding group of pupils enter the room with a repetitive chorus of, 'Miss, it's really hot in here!' Immediately you are on the defensive, so it is worth stepping outside the classroom from time to time during the day, and if the need is there, open the window.

Next... curtains and displays. Yes, the little things count because they all contribute to the big thing; the pupils' subconscious impression of the learning environment. What messages are being sent to the recently arrived pupils? Are the curtains anyhow after the previous group? Are they supposed to be open or closed? All of this helps to create an impression of orderliness, reinforcing that sense that the teacher is in control. Displays: are they neat, tidy and up to date? Pupils will know instinctively if the same display has been up there all year or, even worse, was up there last year or when they first came to the school. Yes, it does happen!

On the other hand, is it only the best work that goes up on the walls? Displays for boffins? Avoid this like the plague. While it's great to display the best work, all of your pupils need to be valued.[33]

One of my first jobs every summer holiday is to take down the old displays and get the backing paper

---

[33] I was the world's worst artist, but I did one year manage to do a half-decent painting of an ocean liner. I cannot tell you the pride I felt on Open Day to see my outstandingly average painting up there! My father slightly detracted from my moment of glory by saying, before he could take a second glance at my masterpiece, 'Shouldn't the funnels be equidistant?' But even that didn't manage to prick my bubble. The fact was that my painting, for once, was up there!

up for the new term's material. It immediately freshens up the room. You won't possibly have time to keep changing every display continuously, but have a plan to change each display board on a rota basis. Good display boards send out powerful subconscious messages which say, 'This teacher knows what she is doing. She is worth behaving for and working hard for.'

Or, depending on how radical you're feeling, set your class a challenge to redecorate your room with this term's topic. Give them a blank wall and tell them, 'That's your wall. In five weeks' time I want it to be the best wall in the school. I want anyone who comes into this class to know about the topic and about you.' You spend three weeks delivering the topic and the last two lessons facilitating what they want to do and allowing them to create the display. You're no longer the teacher. You're the helper. Imagine the learning. And the team work. Plus, they are engaged, enjoying themselves and they learn to trust you. And, fingers crossed, you have a display to die for!

So, you've planned. You've created an environment in which learning can flourish. The next chapter looks at the lesson itself. But before that, settle down for a heart-warming story about the three bears. Are you sitting comfortably?

Top tips

1. Create and environment in which pupils can learn.

2. Check for sights, sounds and smells.

3. Be organised before they come through the door.

Bonus story

And you thought you were busy?

Baby Bear goes downstairs, sits in his small chair at the table. He looks into his small bowl. It is empty. 'Who's been eating my porridge?' he squeaks.

Daddy Bear arrives at the big table and plonks himself in his big chair. He looks into his big bowl and it is also empty. 'Who's been eating my porridge?' he roars.

Mummy Bear puts her head through the serving hatch from the kitchen and yells, 'For God's sake, how many times do I have to go through this with you idiots? It was Mummy Bear who got up first. It was Mummy Bear who woke everyone in the house. It was Mummy Bear who made the coffee. It was Mummy Bear who unloaded the dishwasher from last night and put everything away. It was Mummy Bear who swept the floor in the kitchen. It was Mummy Bear who went out in the cold early morning air to fetch the newspaper and croissants. It was Mummy Bear who set the damn table.'

Daddy Bear was looking at his shoes. Baby Bear's bottom lip was trembling.

'It was Mummy Bear who walked the bloody dog, cleaned the cat's litter tray, gave them their food and refilled their water. And now that you've decided to drag your sorry bear-arses downstairs and grace Mummy Bear with your grumpy presence, listen carefully, because I'm only going to say this once.'

Mummy Bear's veins on her neck were standing out. 'I HAVEN'T MADE THE EFFING PORRIDGE YET!'

Chapter 8

Teaching 1: The perfect start

We are confronted with insurmountable opportunities.

Walt Kelly

In a nutshell

This chapter is about the bleedin' obvious (again). It covers the basics of classroom tactics, which we describe as common sense but by no means common practice. Where do you stand? How should you speak? What's the best way to challenge latecomers? How should you call the register? We offer some cool advice about how to run your most valuable lesson of the year: September, day 1! Experience tells us that it's very difficult to recover if things begin badly, so we focus on starters - to get you off to a flyer. It's all about impact folks, so we conclude with a bonus story about the moon landing the like of which you've probably not heard before.

Yes, you're right, we spent the whole of the last two chapters talking about things to consider *before* you have even started the formal part of the lesson. The 7 Ps indeed! But we are convinced that it is attention to the little things that makes the big things come right.

Let us assume that the pupils have arrived to find a room which is orderly and which shows all the hallmarks of a teacher who knows what they are doing.[34] The next thing to consider is kick-starting the learning as well as dealing with the essential business of the class.

Engagement

Every good lesson has something to engage the attention of the children as soon as they arrive. More about this later, but if they have something wholesome which will lead them into their learning on arrival, it gives you more time and space to do the necessary business as well. Remember, the aim of this book is to give you top tips which will make life easier for you and help you to enjoy your job more. You will feel frazzled enough without the stress that comes from being disorganised!

Think about where you want to be in the classroom. Do you feel more in control sitting or standing? Where should you sit or stand? Some teachers like to be centre stage. Others prefer to be to one side so kids can see the board. Whatever you decide, can you see the kids, all of them, including the ones you particularly want to see? They don't always

---

[34] It seems almost too obvious for words to mention it, but what is the state of your teacher's desk? We preach to our pupils the virtues of good husbandry and good organisation on a daily basis, so what are they to conclude if our desk is in a state of chaos? I once asked a particularly shambolic deputy head for a copy of the Clubs List for my class, to which she replied, 'I think you'll find one on my desk'. My problem was locating her desk under the mountains of accumulated paperwork, never mind the aforementioned Clubs List! Not good!

have to see you, but they need to know you can always see them.

What about calling for order at the beginning of a class? Your most precious asset is your voice, and one of the things which causes most stress to your voice is calling for order, so establish recognised conventions. We have seen teachers who raise one hand in the air, others who use little bells or squeezy whistles, others have luminous toys and when they are held up, that is the signal for everyone to be quiet. A very effective technique is the use of a rhythmic tapping sound, made for instance with a pen or a ruler, where the rhythm slows gradually until it stops. Other techniques include the broken record technique where you say quite quietly, 'Emma, are you ready now? Emma, are you ready now? Emma, are you ready now?' until Emma complies. When she does, thank her and make light of it. She'll be more in tune next time.

You may well be a form or class tutor or may work in a school where an official register is taken electronically every lesson. This is an official document and it is absolutely essential that it is completed accurately. You would not believe how many problems incomplete or inaccurate registers cause. Obvious... and yet, when you are busy keeping order, collecting in bits and pieces, dealing with lateness, answering a knock at the door and all the other myriad things you have to do as a class teacher, it is so easy to forget to put a mark against the child who you were told is here but isn't here, or vice versa. In these days of safeguarding, many schools will have established routines for contacting parents if their child is not in school, and it doesn't look good if the office rings home to report that Joe is away today, only to be told, 'Oh no, what has happened then? He left here at the normal time!' When it turns out that you didn't mark your register correctly, you don't look good!

A well-organised mark book is an essential tool for an efficient teacher. First things first: make sure you have all the names (again, easier said than done as the school year unfolds and new pupils join and others leave). A few years ago a new pupil who arrived one November said to me in July, 'I don't think Miss even knows who I am yet! I'm not even on her register.' Every child matters?

Second, make sure you have the spellings right. Names grow ever more bizarre and yet parents expect you to spell their child's name correctly. Yes, they will make it as difficult as possible for you (how many different ways are there of spelling Jayden or Aimee?) but they will expect you to get it right!

Of course, there are those names that take you completely by surprise and will gradually become part of the amusement your profession has given you over the years. Between us, we've come across Annette Kertain, J Reg Brown (born in 1992 to a car enthusiast!), Matt Black, Scott Land, Teresa Green, Phillip Gap and Miles Long. You will dine out on them for years.[35]

Once these basics are in place you have a decision to make about what to include in your mark book. You can choose to use an electronic, computerised style or you can opt for good old-fashioned columns of information. It is up to you,

---

[35] Andy once taught a class where there was a Mr Lancaster sitting next to a Mr Messerschmitt (100% true).

although you may find the regime in your school guides your choice. Whichever you use, think about what goes in it. It is an indispensable tool for you. It should contain as much information as is available about each child. It is then invaluable to you as you move around the school, attending different meetings or teaching in different areas, and particularly at Parents' Evenings when it can be your greatest asset.

So, here goes as to what information we think you should record:

- Attendance, so that you know which pupils were present when. Nothing will derail a lesson more quickly than a prolonged battle with a child who hasn't produced a piece of work and is claiming they were not there for that lesson. Equally, nothing disarms the professional slackers more readily than to realise that Sir/ Miss has got their finger right on the button.

- Hand in hand with attendance, in your own code that you can understand, a record of who has completed specific pieces of work.

- A record of SEN and medical information - again, I use my own code which reminds me of the important information I need to retain, e.g. who needs the toilet urgently, who has serious medical conditions of which I should be aware and any other factors I need to keep an eye on. I do this in code in case a pupil has a peer at my register, because the privacy of every child is of course paramount.

- Then you will need to have to hand the child's current levels and their target levels. You may well also have a battery of other data, such as reading age, spelling age, cognitive ability scores and so on. You need to organise this so that it is accessible and useful to you.

Don't feel you have to call the register at the outset of the lesson. We have seen many very skilful teachers set the class going on a task and then quite unobtrusively doing the register so that hardly anyone notices. If you do call it out, here's a tip - don't always start with the As and work your way to the Ws. You can win some huge friends among the Wilsons, Woodruffs and Woolmans of this world by starting at their end of the alphabet!

How should children respond to the register? Again the convention of your school should guide you, but whatever is the suggested routine, 'Yea,' or 'Yo' is never a recommended response. It sounds slovenly and disrespectful, and one of the fundamental requirements of our stewardship of these young people while they are in our charge is to prepare them for the grown-up world, and that means showing respect for the person in charge, in other words, good manners.

Latecomers! There can be few more frustrating things, especially with a difficult class, than to get the lesson underway, only to hear that knock at the door and you glance up to see someone, or worse, *more than one*, coming in late. Our best tip is to get them in and settle them as quickly and as calmly as you can, if possible carrying on your teaching while you are doing so.[36] When there is an opportunity

---

[36] What we call 'overlapping', where you are overlapping two tasks. We have resisted the temptation to stereotype the fact that female teachers are able to multi-task whereas male teachers might struggle. Suffice to say that if your male other half is reading the paper, he cannot hear you!

to do so, then go over to those who were late and find out why they were late and make clear what the position is with regard to punctuality. This way you have signalled to the miscreants that you are not a soft touch but equally they have not caused any significant disruption to the class.

Fools rush in?

> *'Rivers know this: there is no hurry. We shall get there some day.'*
>
> **Winnie the Pooh**

And please don't feel obliged to jump straight in with syllabus-driven content. Chill. Maybe your very first morning of the new year is about setting ground rules for behaviours and attitudes. Once again, it depends on how confident you're feeling, but we believe there is significant value in running an activity that asks the children to come up with their own ground rules for behaviour. Maybe the questions are:

1. How are we going to treat each other in this classroom?

2. What is acceptable and unacceptable behaviour in this classroom?

3. What do I expect of Miss?

4. What can Miss expect of me?

5. What do I expect of my fellow learners in this classroom?

6. What kind of attitude serves us best?

7.   What do we want to achieve this term?

Half an hour to think about it in groups; half an hour to feed it back and agree on the key points. They then write it up as a display, add your signature and theirs and, voilà, you have a set of behaviours that the children have signed up to. If they fall out of line the agreement is pinned on the wall, fair and square! In business parlance I think they'd call it 'empowerment'. In the world of education it could well be the most valuable lesson you ever run.

Giving out books, files or whatever written records you operate with is an ideal opportunity to help you learn the names of your pupils, and it is also a brilliant chance to have a mini-conversation with each one. More about this in the next chapter, but finding a moment for each individual is such a useful tool in your armoury.

One of the best pieces of advice I was ever given was to collect in the books open at the right page, ready for marking. You will save yourself up to a third of your marking time because you are not flipping through each book trying to find the right page. This is even more important for those pupils who haven't yet mastered the art of using the pages in a book sequentially. You know the ones I mean, who open the book at random, sometimes even upside down, and start writing!

Many of you will experience the 'forest of hands' syndrome. This is when you say, 'For the next part of the lesson you will need a pencil and a ruler,' and you are greeted by all those hands, along with helpful comments like, 'I ain't got a ruler, Miss!' A well-organised teacher always carries spares with them. If you are itinerant, then a box of essential supplies is well worth the investment.[37]

Starters

Particularly with a difficult class, it is essential that your lesson starts with an activity which they can do successfully. Therefore, top of my list are activities which require putting things in a particular order or sequence, or choosing an odd one out. The virtue of these as lesson starters is that no one can be wrong, so you start with a success story.

Here are a couple of examples to get you thinking:

- If you were teaching about the countries of the European Union, your starter could be to put six countries on the screen or board and ask the pupils to write them down in the order in which they would like to visit them, and then say why. The second bit of course is demanding higher-order thinking skills because they have to 'justify' their decision. Or 'list these countries from North to South' or 'largest to smallest in terms of population', although you have surrendered the principle of 'you can't be wrong'!

- Matching or odd one out activities are always good to get the brain juices flowing, so you could ask pupils to match football players to countries, types of car to countries, types of food to countries, and then of course design

[37] When you are giving out pencils, rulers etc. it's worth counting how many you have given out, write the number on the board, and tell the class how many it is. This beams the unconscious message to them that you are on the ball and they need to remember to give the borrowed item back at the end.

it so you have one left over. Which country do they think that would come from? Make that the lead-in to the learning for the lesson.

With these examples, pupils have ample opportunity to be right, because often there are no correct or incorrect answers, and these activities require almost no prior planning in terms of making time-consuming resources.

'Here are three answers from the last lesson. What were the questions?' is a nice linking activity which provokes creative thought as well, because there could be more than one question which would deliver the answer 'France'.

A couple of starters that require rather more in terms of preparation but which have plenty of mileage include 'circle the mistakes'. They always enjoy 'being the teacher'! Prepare a selection of written answers that contain mistakes, linking it to either prior learning or learning to be developed. The first pupil has to circle the mistakes. Then a second pupil must give the correction and you can challenge them to see if the first pupil has missed anything or has circled something that was in fact correct. It is a very effective technique for testing prior learning and for generating focused and energetic discussion at the beginning of a lesson.

Top tips

1. Start each lesson with something engaging. Aim for a quick win.

2. The register is an official document. Take it seriously.

3. Get to know names asap.

4. Use your mark book to record information about each child.

5. Use lesson 1 to sketch out the ground rules. Don't impose the rules, negotiate them.

Bonus story

To infinity and beyond...

No folks, we've already had *Kung Fun Panda*, *Monsters Inc* and *'The Three Bears'*, so we're changing the theme. This isn't about Buzz Lightyear. It's about Buzz *Aldrin*, world famous for being the... ahem... the second man on the moon! Poor Buzz. Never got over it you see. Some of the following may be urban myth and we've embellished for effect, but please bear with it anyway.

Buzz was actually scheduled to be the first man on the moon. First of all, they were lucky to even get to the moon. Their space ship had less technology than is in a modern day mobile phone. The lunar module overshot its landing site and the computer apparently produced an error message '1202'. No one had ever seen this message before. It wasn't in the manual, which, to be honest, would have worried me a tad as I hurtled toward the surface of the moon. And, on a planet far, far away, 600 million people crowded round their TVs watching and waiting as the guys managed, against the odds, to land the craft. Hurrah! The door opened and out stepped Neil. He said a few iconic words and stepped down to place a human footprint on the lunar landscape. It was a big moment. There had always been a man in the moon but now we had one on it.

And Buzz? Well, he was sulking. He lingered on the steps for an eternity. Six hundred million people wondered why. Fear? Overcome by emotion? No. If my research is to be believed, he was doing a wee in his spacesuit! (I guess it personalises it. Same principle as doing one in your wetsuit?) Anyway, he refused to take a pic of Neil. In Derby parlance, we'd say 'he had a bag on'.

To cut a long story short, the guys wandered around, played a bit of zero-gravity golf and went home. I was only three so can't really remember it, but my dad tells me the media attention was huge. The Apollo photos revealed the insignificance of the earth - a tiny marble lost in an eternity of blackness. On the moon Armstrong discovered he could eclipse earth merely by raising his thumb. 'Did it make you feel really big?' asked an enthusiastic reporter. 'No, it made me feel really small,' replied Neil, which I always think is a cool reply.

Armstrong remained stable after going to the moon. In fact, he's still around, doing guest lectures and corporate events. Buzz, on the other hand, sank into depression and alcoholism.

Look, I don't know the exact facts. The above is said with an attempt at humour and with a little bit of reading between the lines. But I reckon Buzz could have played his hand differently. He could have been second down the ladder and stood on the moon like a 2%er. 'Woohooo!' While Neil was poncing for photos, Buzz could have done a Jacko moonwalk or a bit of disco. Or, even better, he could have ruined Neil's photo with the old rabbit ears trick. He could have high-fived his mate and leaped around like he was from another planet. While Neil was boring the pants off people with his 'first step for man...' speech, Buzz could have knelt down, picked up a rock, beamed at camera 3 and said, 'it really is made of cheese'. He would have had no need to feel depressed. And we'd have remembered Buzz differently. He wouldn't have been sidelined forever as 'second man on the moon', he'd have been elevated to 'best man on the moon'.

The lesson? Make your mark folks. Be a model of enthusiasm and positivity. Be remembered for all the *right* reasons!

Chapter 8

Teaching 2: Engagement

'If the person you are talking to doesn't appear to be listening, be patient. It may simply be that he has a small piece of fluff in his ear.'

Winnie the Pooh

In a nutshell

An eclectic mix of business theory and classroom practice, ending with a tearjerker! The pyramid below gets us off to an interesting start and Andy tries to make out that education is just like Tesco! Mmmm, not sure teachers will go for that? We move swiftly on to talk about energy, Vauxhall Vivas and radio wavelengths. Yoof culture gets a big mention and we stress the importance of engaging your learners. This chapter goes on to give oodles of examples to get your juices flowing and ends with a heart-warming story that will get your tears flowing.

Every little helps

Time for one of Andy's business models. And, look, it's a pyramid! *Whooppee!*

This is unashamedly taken from the commercial world. And, I appreciate that the word 'customers' is anathema to many teachers, but I believe this model warrants at least sixty seconds of your time. In the competitive business world (which, it is very easy to argue, your school is in) we are aiming to get to the top of the pyramid. Tesco would probably call this 'customer loyalty'; it means shoppers come back again and again and they have an affinity for the brand. As advocates, they are likely to speak highly of you and the good word spreads. In the business world they would call it 'viral marketing' and it's exactly the same in your school. The word is out there folks. I don't want you to become any more paranoid than you already are, but they're talking about you... and I'm sure you'd rather they be saying fabulous things!

All 'businesses' need to start at the bottom of the hierarchy, as do you as a classroom teacher. You need to know who your pupils are. Then you need to ascertain what they want from you - generally, that you have some control and you teach them something. Then, you need to meet their requirements, i.e. give them what they expect.

Good classroom teachers go further, reaching level 4, exceeding expectations. Perhaps they make the lessons enjoyable along the way?

Super-teachers nail the first four levels and also attack the top three. They are ahead of the game. Not only are they exceeding expectations in the 'here and now', they are scanning the environment, looking for ways to enhance next week, next month and next year. They are consistently alert for ways and means to enhance the classroom experience. In short, they reach the Nirvana of 'gaining commitment', and that does indeed translate to 'customer loyalty'. In the business world we would say that your customers are not just purchasing goods or services from you, they are buying the whole experience of dealing with you and your business. Once again, I think this translates perfectly to the world of education. It's not just what you teach, it's how you teach it. You come as a whole package. 'Customer loyalty' arises when children come to your class because they want to. There is no dragging of feet and 'please Miss can I go to the toilet'. Homework comes in on time. Their grades for you are better than their grades elsewhere. Their behaviour is good to excellent. There is good-natured banter. These are you advocates and they will be talking fondly of you thirty years from now.

So, I hear you ask, how do we reach this Nirvana world of pupils skipping to your lessons and knuckling down to some world-class learning?[38]

Entropy

> *For fast acting relief, try slowing down.*
>
> **Anonymous**

First things first - teaching requires energy. Many teachers spend their weekends recovering before they plunge back into the mania of the working week. Andy calls it 'busyness'. This means there aren't enough hours in the day to accomplish what you want to achieve. So you end up getting to work a bit earlier and staying a bit later. Plus, work comes home with you. And there are reports to write and meetings to attend and an apparent onslaught of parents' evenings. We're living life fast, but are we living it well? Incidentally, 'busyness' is an epidemic across society. It's by no means unique to teaching.

Busyness saps our energy. If you're a science teacher you might be aware of the term 'entropy'. If you'll allow me to gloss over the detail, entropy is all about energy. Over time, energy seeps away. For example, in 1973 my dad had a Vauxhall Viva. It was his pride and joy. He would spend every Sunday T-Cutting it so the bodywork shone and the chrome bumpers dazzled. Then, one day, my dad came home in a new car - an Austin Maxi. I was seven at the time but, believe you me, I knew that was a bad move. I have very strong memories of dad's Maxi - green with a brown vinyl roof. In those days you had to run an engine in. This means that you weren't allowed to

---

[38] I might be laying it on a tad thick here? But we can all dream!

go more than 30 mph for the first 5000 miles. Imagine? And the first thing we did was go on holiday to Cornwall. At 30 mph. From Derby! It took four days!

I digress... To cut a long story short, my dad never managed to sell his Viva. So his former pride and joy sat on the driveway for three years. And if you looked at the Viva you'd have seen it gradually sagging as its tyres went flat. The grass grew up around it. Its shining cherry bodywork turned to a drab pinky/orange. And those dazzling bumpers developed blisters of rust. The Viva even developed a dent in its bumper (which I always describe as self-harming). The Viva's energy was slipping away.

And, you see, the same can happen to teachers and classrooms! Enthusiastic teachers can become battle-weary. NQTs can lose their lustre very quickly. This is when we start to succumb to 'destination addiction' (counting down, wishing the weeks away to half term).[39]

Here are some classic signs of what we call 'classroom entropy', where the energy will be seeping from your lessons:

- no longer having time for celebration

- problem-makers outnumber problem-solvers

- bad planning means the lesson gets off to a poor start

- meetings are always about problems

- when there's a new starter you think, 'I used to be as enthusiastic as that!'

---

[39] I once met a teacher aged thirty-five whose catchphrase was 'only twenty-five years to go!'

- too many people have that 'here we go again' feeling

- teachers speak of pupils as impositions on their time rather than opportunities to serve

- focus is on surviving the week

- focus is on systems rather than people.

You can probably think of more, but these are classic signs that energy is dissipating. If you're guilty of any, our advice is to remedy your behaviour immediately. Teachers need to create energy, not let it seep away. In fact, it's useful to think of your lesson as an opportunity for an 'immense infusion of energy'. How can you breathe life into even the dullest of subject matter so that your most reluctant learner is engaged? That is our challenge as teachers. If we do not connect with our learners, learning will not happen. I am always mindful of some words of wisdom from Confucius: 'A wise man catches more flies with honey than with vinegar!' Otherwise we are into Syrup of Figs territory, where you force-feed unpleasant medicine down their throats, telling them that it is good for them. Ok, so you might successfully be able to ram a certain amount of learning down their necks, but I am going to entice you into thinking that there is a better way.

On the right wavelength?

> When you're chewing on life's gristle, don't grumble, give a whistle! And this'll help things turn out for the best. Always look on the bright side of life...
>
> **Monty Python**

First let us think of my favourite radio station, Radio WiiFM. It's the one every young learner is tuned into. Radio **W**hat's **i**n **i**t **F**or **M**e?

What is there in your lesson that is going to give answers to the question, 'Why should I behave for him/her? Why should I work in this lesson? What is there in it for me?'

How often do we find ourselves desperately trying to force onto children parts of the syllabus which they really aren't interested in and don't want to buy into?

'Why do we have to learn this Miss?'

You answer, in exasperated tones, 'because it's on the syllabus and it might crop up in the exam'. And, of course, we have immediately doomed the subject to being irrelevant to anything other than a school examination. The kids roll their eyes and you spend an hour force-feeding them GCSE or SATs fodder.

So, what are the tricks of the trade? We need to start from the assumption that the kids you are teaching do not bring with them, over the threshold of your classroom, any intrinsic interest in what you are trying to teach them. You may, of course, think that your wunderlesson on how to use a semicolon is riveting stuff but, in all honesty, it is not big in terms of conversation at the local chippy. You may be fascinated by the intricacies of photosynthesis but I would be surprised if it was a massive conversation piece among teenagers down the park in the evenings. So how do we make these things come alive for them?

Yoof culture

First, let us think of their own 'kid culture'. How can we connect with their world? What are the things they are interested in?

Take football as an example. How could that be used in a lesson? Teaching about primary colours in a primary school classroom or colours in a foreign language could easily be linked with football teams. A little research would almost certainly reveal fixture lists for your local club that would enable you to explore where the other teams are, in this country or in Europe. This could lend itself to numeracy work on distances or times for travel. Information about players' ages and birthdays again could easily lend itself to numeracy work, and on the literacy front, it could lead to work on comparatives and superlatives (older, oldest etc.).

I started a series of lessons on Romeo and Juliet by waving £30 in front of the class (flashing the cash always catches their attention). I asked them what they would rather do, spend it going to watch their local football team on a Saturday or going to Stratford to watch Romeo and Juliet. The reply was of course predictable, and exactly what I wanted, so I followed it up with, 'So why will there be empty seats in the footie stadium on Saturday, while this play sells out night after night after night, over 400 years after it was written, when everyone knows the story? What is so special about it?' Total silence. They were hooked by the challenge. I had got them where I wanted them to explore Shakespeare's play.

What about television? What do they watch? How can you make use of their favourite TV programmes to get them on board? You can use the format of well-known TV shows in your lessons. At the time of writing, shows that involve an element of competition with judges and a telephone vote are all the rage. Kids love being judges. So, when your class have completed whatever exercise you have given them, make them present their work to the class and have three judges. This is brilliant for engaging hard-to-reach kids. They love being the judge. You will need to give them guidance about what the criteria are for judging, otherwise there is always the opportunity for them to give a bad verdict because they don't like whoever has just presented their work. I am very particular about this. You can even have fun ways of them registering their verdict on the performance. I have cards with a Ferrari, a Ford Fiesta and a Noddy car for judges to use, or on another lesson I have two cards, one with Champagne and the other with Lager. I invite the judges to say whether the contestant they have just seen is a Champagne Charlie or a Lager Lout.

Now you are broadcasting right on their wavelength, channel WiiFM.

There are other formats you can borrow and adapt. Good starters can be made with 'Who Wants to be a Millionaire' type questions and, of course, let them phone a friend or go 50:50 if they want. 'Countdown', 'Deal or no Deal', 'Family Fortunes' are all good. The list goes on, and yes, I'm sorry, but it does mean that you watch TV yourself with half of your subconscious mind scanning every programme for usable formats for your lessons!

Children will always enjoy pitting their wits against either you or each other. A really good plenary is to put a brown envelope on the board at the beginning of the lesson containing three facts from the lesson you are about to deliver. For example, with a class who have been studying Roman emperors, you could put three emperors in the envelope. You can spice it up by asking them to guess the names in the same order you have written them so, for example, you could write them in the order of how long they were emperor. If they win, they win whatever prize is the currency of your school. And, by the way, because you are asking them to guess three, they don't usually get it, so if you have been brave enough to offer a chocolate bar, you often end up eating it yourself. Result!

Games against the clock are always popular. So in a languages lesson at primary or secondary school, ask pupils to name all the numbers on the board in under a minute. For all games like that it works really well if you have got a stopwatch. Plus, this can be a great way of ensuring the involvement of some hard-to-engage pupils. Get them to be the timer.

'I bet...' is always a challenge that gets them going, particularly boys. 'I bet you couldn't name ten elements in under thirty seconds...; ten adjectives ending in -ible' or whatever your subject matter is. Again, have rewards at the ready.

What is there in your lesson that is memorable? When the kids sit down in their family home that evening and mum asks them, 'What did you do at school today?' what is there in your lesson which will make them say, 'Oh it was brilliant in Miss So and So's lesson...'?

I taught with a colleague once who had a reputation for dancing on the tables. He assures me he only ever did it twice in his entire career but boy, did his kids remember those lessons! A very popular English teacher I taught with had a reputation for bursting into song mid-lesson in a variety of styles: full-scale operatic, pop songs with adapted words, little ditties etc. It helps if you have a reputation for being slightly off the wall, a little bit zany, that little bit different from all their other teachers. Sometimes you can be just that little bit shocking. The spoof phone call is always a favourite. I have a colleague who has an array of phones from mobiles to old-fashioned models, and his lessons are frequently interrupted by an imaginary caller, sometimes with a saucy innuendo thrown in!

Amazing facts can spice up a lesson. A lesson on reading which had a PowerPoint showing the world's oldest book, biggest book, longest book is the sort of thing that always gets the attention of the learner. I guess that is the trick. What we are all trying to do is to lock onto their radar so that we can impart the priceless gems of learning that are in our lesson plans! [40]

---

[40] One of your best friends is the Guinness Book of Records.

Bringing in artefacts that link to the learning gets right to the heart of the matter. In a lesson where Roald Dahl's Boy was being read, the teacher used his fantastic description of an old-fashioned sweetshop. She not only brought in a variety of the same old-fashioned sweets to be tasted and described using similes and metaphors, but also the full range of old pre-decimal coinage to put it in context.

Children work best and learn best when they want to. Getting children to want to do what you want them to do is always your best trick. This is a Y generation; they want to know why they are doing a particular task, so give them an audience and give them a context. Of course it can be entirely fictitious.

Baron Von Munchausen is sitting in his castle and has offered a huge reward to those who can do today's science experiment correctly!

Or...

The three-toed aliens in their space ship have promised not to invade Earth if everybody learns three things about gravity today.

Be creative. Position yourself at the 'slightly mad' end of the staffroom spectrum. Fire the kids imaginations, lead from the front, blow their minds and they will follow you. They will do exactly what you want of them, they will be fiercely loyal to you and, above all, they will learn. That is the most rewarding feeling in the world.

> *There is nothing noble about being superior to some other man. The true nobility is in being superior to your previous self.*
>
> **Hindu proverb**

The trick is to make connections between what is happening in the children's lives and what you are hoping to teach them. You know those kids and what they are about because you teach them day in, day out. You know what makes them tick. No visiting inspector or any other important person who parachutes into your classroom knows them half as well as you do, so make the most of it.

Before this section ends, let's just remind you again of an early challenge we posed. Your challenge is to get to know each child; that means get to know their name, get to know something about them and, above all, get to know how to make them laugh. Get these things right and you will have them eating out of your hand and, coincidentally, they will experience giant leaps of learning. Oh, and you will enjoy coming to work every day as well. That's important too.

Top tips

1. Plan to exceed expectations.

2. Eat the right things. Exercise daily. Teaching is exhausting so you need to be on top form.

3. Tune into Radio WiiFM. Ask yourself, why should kids want to turn up to my lesson?

4. Scan the youth culture environment for activities and references. Make the learning relevant.

5. Position yourself at the 'whacky' end of the staffroom spectrum, way above the most boring member of staff and just below the staff nutter (let's face it, you can be too enthusiastic!).

Bonus story[41]

A few weeks ago I met a guy who had been working as a consultant in the supermarket industry. He had one of those mouth wateringly impressive clients who asked him to transform their customer service programme. Basically, his remit was to develop an ethos that would build customer loyalty.

So, he did what all consultants do. He charged a fortune to tell them what they already knew and offered some training to hone their skills. He focused his attention on the bottom quartile of stores. There was one in particular that was underperforming and he conducted some training that culminated in what, in his own words, he describes as, 'one of those rousing Churchillian speeches peppered with a few clichés.'

'Such as?' I asked.

'I said every single one of them could make a difference. I challenged them to create memories for their customers that will motivate them to come back.'

'Punching the air?' I grimaced.

'I'm afraid so,' he admitted. 'And I finished with the statement, "go and put your personal signature on the job".'

---

[41] Shamelessly borrowed and embellished, but true nevertheless.

Ouch! I thought. *Sounds a bit 'David Brent' to me.* And, as is typical with consultants, he failed to tell them exactly how to put their signature on their job - just sort of left them to work it out for themselves.

Anyway, about a month later he received a call from a 19-year-old packer called Jimmy. He proudly informed my consultant chum that he had Down's Syndrome. And he had a story to tell...

'I liked what you talked about,' said Jimmy. 'But I couldn't think of how I could do anything special for our customers. You see, I'm only a bag packer. Then I had an idea! Every night after work I'd come home and find a thought for the day. If I couldn't find a saying I liked I'd just make one up.'

It transpired that Jimmy's dad then helped him type his thought for the day into the computer and they'd print off multiple copies. Jimmy then cut out each quote and signed the back. Then he'd pack them in his bag so he wouldn't forget to take them to work.

'And when I finish bagging someone's shopping,' he explained, 'I put my thought for the day in their bag and say ,'Thanks for shopping with us today.'

'That's lovely,' I cooed. 'Nice one Jimmy.' But apparently it doesn't stop there.

A month later the store manager phoned. 'You won't believe what's happened! When I was out on the shop floor, doing my rounds, I found Jimmy's checkout had a massive queue. It was three times longer than the others. So, obviously, good customer service means that I quickly opened up some more tills to try and get the customers through more quickly. But, get this... none of them wanted to move. They wouldn't budge. In fact, one woman got a bit shirty with me. 'I want to be in Jimmy's aisle,' she said. 'I want his thought for the day.' Another customer explained that he used to come shopping once a week but he now comes every day because he doesn't want to miss out on Jimmy's thought for the day.'

Two months later the manager called again. His store was no longer bottom of the league tables. He'd just won an award for being top! 'Jimmy has transformed our store. Now, when the floral department has a broken flower they find an elderly lady or little girl and pin it on their blouse. Everyone's having fun creating memories. Our customers are talking about us. They're grinning. They're coming back and bringing their friends. A wonderful spirit of service has spread throughout the entire store - and all because Jimmy chose to make a difference.'

And here's the thought; Jimmy's clearly a 2%er. I think teachers are perfectly placed to make a difference. What can you do, extra, that will make someone's day?

Chapter 9

Teaching 3:
The grand finale

Look, I don't want to wax philosophic, but I will say that if you're alive you've got to flap your arms and legs, you've got to jump around a lot, for life is the very opposite of death, and therefore you must at very least think noisily and colourfully, or you're not alive.

Mel Brookes

In a nutshell

All good things must come to an end, and so must your world-class lessons. You started with a bang, engaged them in the middle bit and are going to finish with a flourish! This section looks exclusively as plenaries, 'thunks' and how to end your day on a glorious high. It's crammed full of practical ideas and finishes with a bonus story that shows just how powerful learning can be.

So, finally for this section, how will your lesson end? A vital ingredient of a super-lesson is a plenary activity that draws together and reinforces what the pupils have learned.

Remember that a plenary does not have to be at the end of a lesson. Indeed, it is good practice to insert mini-plenaries into the course of your lesson. Making a general statement here, young males have notoriously short attention spans, and learning will take place much more effectively if your lesson is chunked into bite-sized pieces, with a mini-plenary at the end of each section which constitutes a building block for the lesson which will add up to a whole.

Before we give you loads of examples of how to end a lesson, let's ram home the importance of plenaries (in case the penny hasn't dropped). Have you ever asked someone about their holiday? You know, they've just come back from Spain so it's only polite to ask. 'How was Marbella?'

'It was superb. Lovely apartment right by the sea. And we went to the most fantastic fish restaurant on the Wednesday.'

And then, guaranteed, you will get this, 'But it clouded over on the last day and the flight home was delayed by forty minutes.'

Your lessons are a bit like that holiday story, in that people will remember the highlight and the last bit. So, please don't ignore the plenary. It will be one of the bits they are *guaranteed* to remember!

Here are enough examples to sink a battleship. Again, we are starting with activities that require minimal preparation in terms of resources.

- 'There are two things I want you to do before the end of the lesson. The second one is pack away, but the first is to tell your partner two things we have learned [you can be specific about the learning aims here] in this lesson.'

Obviously the exact component of the task can be adapted, but the principle is sound, especially because as soon as you spot someone packing away, you go up to them and ask what they decided were the two things they had learned.

- You can simplify this by asking each pair to agree on five things they have learned in the lesson, and then asking them to decide which two were the most important so that they can report to the class. Again this fosters thinking skills, which reinforces learning.

- This can be taken a stage further by dividing the class down the middle. One half thinks of an answer from today's lesson, while the others think of a question. You then pick a pupil with an answer first, so he or she might say 'Pudding Lane', and you then pick another pupil with a question, so he or she might say, 'What year was the great fire of London?' Clearly you don't have a match but you can offer rewards for the first pair randomly chosen to get a match.

- A plenary which requires some more advanced thinking skills but which always extends learning is to ask, 'In what other context could you apply what we have learned today?' So, if you have been working on dictionary skills, you could use the same skills to use a foreign language dictionary or you could use alphabetisation to find names in a telephone directory. If you had been using a mnemonic to remember the colours of the rainbow or the order of the planets, you could use the same technique to remember the order of Tudor and Stuart Kings, noble gases or books in the Bible.

- 'Stand up, sit down' is another cracker. Let's assume we've been learning Spanish months: each pupil will choose a month. The teacher calls out clues, e.g. the third month, the month after September etc. and if it is your month, you have to sit down, and you see who is the last one standing.

- Pupils love games against the clock, particularly boys because it appeals to their competitive instinct, e.g. how many questions can they answer in one minute? Items to name, as in the TV programme 'Question of Sport', are always successful in engaging your learners, especially when they are vying to beat each other by achieving an even faster time. Pair up shy or reluctant learners to ensure they are engaged too.

- The brown envelope on the board (which we briefly covered earlier) is another ploy which can be relied upon to engage attention. At the beginning of the lesson, attach an envelope containing three answers from today's lesson to the board at the front, so that pupils see that there is no way you could tamper with it. At the end of a lesson on, for instance, the wives of Henry VIII, you tell them that the names of three of the wives are written on a piece of paper in the envelope. If they can write down the correct three in the right order, they will get a Commendation, Merit, Gold Star or whatever. In my experience they very rarely get the answer once you have stipulated that it must be in the right order, but they love trying to outwit you.

- 'Hot seating' is a drama-style activity that can be used and adapted for all sorts of different situations. A pupil comes to the front and has to sit on a chair or stool and they answer questions from the class, imagining that they are a particular person. So, they might be Henry VIII and other pupils can ask them questions that they must answer as Henry VIII. The first question might be, 'Tell us about your first wife.' The answer might be, 'Well, we got on well to begin with, although she only spoke Spanish when she first arrived...'. You will have to make a judgement about your class with this activity. You can let the pupils make up their own questions, given the usual guidance on good taste, or you may decide to prepare questions on cards which can then be chosen at random. This can be adapted so that you introduce an expert on the content of the lesson. For example, Professor Ludwig van Whistlehofen, who is a world expert on carbon dioxide, the Normans, textile dying, making websites or whatever is the focus of your lesson. The others have to ask relevant questions of the invited guest.

- You could use the same idea of prepared questions, but this time pupils must choose a question on a lucky dip basis and they must answer their question. You can, of course, introduce scoring systems to suit your class, so they can get one point if they can answer the question themselves or they can pass it to someone else as a challenge. If that pupil can't answer it correctly, the first person gets two points, but if the question is answered correctly, a point is deducted from the person who passed it on. Remember, engagement is the name of the game!

- 'Yes/No', where children must answer your questions without using either 'Yes' or 'No' can be a good one, but it does require a certain amount of intellectual dexterity on the part of the teacher to frame the questions appropriately!

- Any format which replicates 'Millionaire' will always be well received and, of course, the kids know all the catchphrases like 'phone a friend', 'go 50:50' and so on. Again, you have used kid culture to engage them - all these game show formats will resonate with them.

Entertaining as all of these activities are, the prime aim is, of course, to consolidate learning. There may well be some interchange between starters and plenaries, but the important thing is to remember the importance of a good start and a good finish to each and every lesson.

Something up your sleeve?

Super-teachers always have something up their sleeve for the end of the lesson. We have all known that feeling when you glance at the clock and suddenly panic because you think you haven't prepared enough. It is always good practice to have an extra activity up your sleeve in case you run short. A refinement of this is to have something at your fingertips as a filler in case you are caught 'waiting for the bell'. The worst day for this is always the day after the clocks have changed and the caretaker has mistakenly put the clock in your classroom two minutes fast. We have all been there. The kids are all standing up, ready to go on time, bags packed, looking at the door... and nothing happens! You have now exhausted your spontaneous pep talk, off-the-cuff mini-conversations and final recap of the lesson, and still the bell hasn't rung!

I particularly like to throw in a few 'thought grenades' or 'thunks'[42]. These are ideal to generate creativity and fun and can be used at the start of the lesson or as a filler at the end. Thunks are designed to engage everyone in thinking. Crucially, they don't have a right or wrong answer. Some of my favourites are:

- What colour is Tuesday?

- Is there more future or past?

- If zebras took over the world, what changes would we see?

- Can you touch the wind?

- If you could take a pill that would make you always happy, would you?

A little weird in places, but that's the whole point. Don't use them all in one lesson. Your students will come to love thunks, so tempt them with, 'If you work brilliantly today and you get your heads round the key points on the board, I have a brilliant thunk for you later.'

If you're feeling really brilliant you can create your own, to tie in with your subject. For example:

- Geography: If a new city were invented, what would you call it? And why?

---

[42] *The Little Book of Thunks* (Ian Gilbert) has hundreds of them! Highly recommended.

- Physics: Newton's mum said her son was the third-best scientist in the world. Who are the others in the top five and why?

- Maths: What would the world be like if maths hadn't been invented?

- Maths: Can you count halfway to infinity?

- IT: Where is the internet?

- Citizenship: Is it ever possible to learn nothing?

- Any subject: Your mum thinks this subject is boring. What would you say/do to prove her wrong?

- History: If the answer is 'Sir Walter Raleigh and a potato', what is the question?[43]

However, you must also beware overrunning at the end of the lesson! Again, it is an elementary error but, once that bell has gone, it is no good saying that the children were restless while you were still setting their homework. They are right and you are wrong. Once the bell has gone, it is their time not yours. Certainly remind them that you are in control and they will leave when you say so, but trying to teach after the official end of the lesson is counterproductive, and they will lose respect for you if it becomes a habit. They don't like being the last to assembly week after week, or being told off in their next class because you always overrun.

As the children leave your classroom, don't pass up the opportunity of mini-conversations. Remember,

---

[43] Those are off the top of my head and, I have to say, were surprisingly easy to create.

this is what your discipline is founded on. Particularly with the hard-to-reach brigade, this is an ideal moment, as they pass you by, to say something positive to them when they don't have the rest of the gallery in attendance. When you see them for the last time in a week or before a break, wish them an enjoyable weekend or holiday.

Finally for this section, make sure that at the end of the last lesson of the day you know what the conventions are for how you should leave the classroom. This can be trickier than you think. In our school, cleaners on one side of the school like the chairs to be up on tables while their colleagues on the other side like them to be down. Tricky stuff! At the end of the day, it is common courtesy and good manners to check that everything is bedded down for the night. Check that the computer is switched off, that your windows are closed and that your lights are off. Caretakers are invaluable allies, but they will soon take umbrage if they are expected to close windows on a summer's evening, and they will not be amused to be called out in the middle of the night because your lights were left on in midsummer, which nobody noticed until it got dark. Again, these are simple courtesies but super-teachers get them right, which makes them good colleagues to work with.

And if you have a time by which all staff should be out of the building, sometimes reinforced by a bell, that means you should be out. It isn't fair on caretakers who work incredibly hard and who do long hours to say, as they go past jangling their keys, 'Give me ten minutes.'

Top tips

1. Finish your lesson with a flourish.

2. Always have something up your sleeve for an awkward moment.

3. Don't overrun.

4. Leave your classroom tidy.

Bonus (true) story

Delivering positive psychology to young people can be challenging. I find myself slipping into sounding like my dad and offering fatherly wisdom or, even worse, losing my rag and ranting at the teenagers. I become a caricature of myself. I care so much, I really do. I tell them. I plead with them. 'You have to change before it's too late!' Sometimes the only future I can envisage involves them appearing on Jeremy Kyle.

Recently I changed my approach. Sounds very odd but I now work much less hard and achieve much better results! I do a very simple activity that asks teenagers to write two short accounts of their life in ten years' time - one if they've lived as a negative mood hoover and one from the perspective of having lived as a positive 2%er. Simplicity. And, I might add, genius. Because it means they are allowed to work it out for themselves. No more ranting required!

Check this out, from Hannah, aged fifteen, from Stoke:

The next 10 years as 'bog standard' Hannah. This is what I see, hear and feel...

I feel tired and ratty! I hear constant nagging in my ear hole like a drill. I stare at four walls and an empty room, I look out the window and see a litter filled street with no normal people, everyone alcoholic or filled from scars from drug usage. I don't have a job, no one will take me, I always relied on dole - it isn't as good as I thought, not at all. I don't have friends any more, I've lost my personality. People would describe me as a serious low life. I didn't achieve and I don't lead in any kind of lifestyle. I am officially depressed.

As a top 2%er. This is what I see, hear and feel...

Smiles, people smiling and laughing. Money's a joke, I could roll around in notes and leave them there. I can hear traffic from the busy streets of the city outside, laughter. I feel good, as always. I live as a film director, life is now my movie, I make it how I like. I'm with the cast and crew writing more film ideas. People would look at me with the look of satisfaction, I am successful. I achieved my dream. What life style do I live? My own.

By Jove, I think she's got it!

Part 3

Discipline

Are we nearly there yet? Yes folks, we are. But we can't arrive at our destination of 'super-teacher' without travelling the treacherous road of discipline. In our metaphoric world of journeys, 'discipline' is one of those mountain passes that we've seen on a Top Gear Special; steep, narrow, slippery and with a sheer drop. One mistake, one lapse of concentration and we're done for!

Discipline is so important we've given it a whole section all of its own. And it's not an exact science. Discipline depends on you, your style, your accepted tolerance levels, the school environment and the pupils. Most people are aware of 'chaos theory', which basically means the flapping of a butterfly's wings in the Amazon somehow affects us. We think 'discipline' is a subset of chaos theory. It's affected by bizarre stuff like the weather, non-uniform day and what was on TV last night. We think it's probably somehow linked to that damned Brazilian butterfly!

But there are some golden rules and top tips. Strap yourself in for a bumpy ride.

10. Have you got your discipline yet?

11. The class from hell

Chapter 10

Have you got your discipline yet?

'Pooh, if you ever need me and I'm not around, you must remember this: You're braver than you believe and stronger than you seem and cleverer than you think.'

Christopher Robin

In a nutshell

Discipline is a bit like the common cold. It wears you down. It's infectious. It makes you want to stay in bed. And nobody's found a cure! This first chapter on discipline looks at Chris's close encounter with an Education Minister and examines both ends of the discipline spectrum. We compare the 'chalk' of the teaching recruitment brochure with the 'cheese' of the real world! This chapter focuses on what we call 'low-level discipline'; the day-to-day nagging issues that all teachers need to keep on top of. We look at relationships, mini-conversations and seating plans. We introduce the oh-so-true 'Matthew Effect' and look at what happens when we get discipline wrong. The chapter is tailed, as always, with something a bit quirky. This time we borrow a famous story from *Chicken Soup for the Soul*. Heart warming indeed.

Yes, Minister

This chapter deals with low-level disruption and how to organise yourself and your classroom to create an environment in which the children know that this is your classroom and you are in charge. The real hard nuts are cracked in the next chapter.

> *The first and greatest commandment is, 'Don't let them scare you'.*
>
> **Elmer Davis**

I have had a recurrent nightmare for the last thirty years... well, all right, not every night, but it has certainly terrified me on a far-too-regular basis: I dream that I have lost control of the class, and you know how it is in a dream, the more you shout and rant the more out of control the situation becomes. And, as is typical of bad dreams, I sometimes want to shout but nothing actually comes out, leaving me feeling even more helpless! 'Ricky, please put that chair down. And, Stacey, please stop dunking Riannah's head in the sink...'. It is with blessed relief that I wake up. Oh bliss! It hasn't really happened. Has it?

There won't be a teacher reading this who hasn't had an awful class. Or a particular group of students that drags your whole day down to the depths of despair.

I remember, when I had been teaching for about a month, meeting an austere and diminutive lady who had, once upon a time, been an Education Minister. I will spare you the details of how I came to be in such company; suffice to say that she frightened me witless. Rarely have I felt so inadequate. From all of 5'2" she fixed me with a beady stare and said, in a threatening tone, 'Have you got your discipline yet?' I gibbered inconsequentially for a moment or two, before I managed somehow to complete a sentence.

Have I got my discipline yet? As though that magic thing called 'discipline' was something you could pluck from a tree or maybe order through a mail-order catalogue? If only! I was teaching in a challenging secondary school in the Midlands and frankly, no, I hadn't 'got my discipline yet'!

Discipline spectrum

Experience of classroom observations suggests that some teachers are willing to tolerate levels of indiscipline that other teachers would find abhorrent. Like everything else in this book, discipline is not an exact science. Some teachers are pally with the students while others like to remain cool. Some are completely aloof and seem to treat pupils as an irritant to their day. Some tolerate backchat, some don't. You don't have to try to be like anyone else. You need to work out what is acceptable and unacceptable in your classroom and then stick to it, consistently.

In fact, if this chapter were to have a key word, it would be 'consistency'. Pupils need to know what the rules of your jungle are and that you'll apply them to every pupil in every situation.

And it's well worth recognising that discipline is a whole-school issue. It is massively beneficial if teachers work as a united team. So, for example, it's very hard for you to uphold the standard of uniforms and to get the difficult Year 11 girls to take off their coats in class if the teacher down the corridor is turning a blind eye; or for you to confiscate mobile phones if the art teacher is allowing in-lesson Facebook chatter.

Harry S. Truman got it exactly right - the disciplinary buck stops with the senior leadership team. But don't underestimate the part you play in setting the tone.

In any school there is a spectrum of discipline. At one end we have a dictator-style 'rule by fear' teacher with a zero-tolerance policy. And at the other extreme, some laissez-faire surfer dude whose classroom is so relaxed as to be horizontal.

Modern-world discipline is a complex art that lies somewhere between the two.

The right mix?

I am going to suggest to you that the magic ingredient called 'discipline' is an inexact recipe. While we certainly don't want to duck the issue, we can't claim to have all the answers. There are a thousand and one things that go into the mixing bowl before you end up with a Mr Kipling-style 'exceedingly good' lesson, which, to anyone visiting your class, looks exactly like it does in the teacher recruitment brochure. You know the one I mean? Smiling teenagers, all with their hands raised, fingers pointing skyward, eager anticipation etched on their faces as they seek to impress Miss with their knowledge of *Lord of the Flies*. Or primary children, dressed in freshly ironed gingham uniforms and adorned with big grins as they enthusiastically engage in making a papier-mâché Eiffel Tower.

And in the politically correct world of the teacher training brochure there's at least one child of each colour and the teacher looks fresh as a daisy. There's probably a slogan, 'Teachers Change Lives'. Sign me up![44]

Just as the picture in the cookbook doesn't always match the cake, the brochure can be misleading. To stretch the cooking metaphor just a little too far, I can add all the right ingredients but my soufflé can still sag in the middle! Annoyingly, you can do the best preparation, have the best start and plan for the most thrilling, engaging lesson in the world, and things can still go wrong. As they say in Yorkshire, 'There's now't as queer as folk'. One pupil can kick off, or the back table can become bored. Or Daniel just doesn't get it. Or Gina's dad stormed out last night and she's emotionally wrecked. Or Leroy falls asleep. Or you have to cover a class and there's no work set for them so you walk into chaos.[45]

Let's go back to the fundamental demands that kids make of you; that you control them and that you teach them something. The bonus comes if they (and you!) enjoy the experience.

Yes, some will make it as challenging as possible for you, to see whether you can hack it, but once you have passed through that pain barrier, you will start to inspire in them a sense of loyalty which

---

[44] In this world of disclaimers ('Lines are now closed. Your vote will not be counted but may still be charged.') I think we need a disclaimer for that glossy brochure. 'The reality may not match the picture. Lessons can be variable and teacher morale can go up as well as down.' Or, more directly, 'Beware! Some kids will drive you to drink.'

[45] Or, on a really bad day, all of the above!

we believe is a key part of maintaining discipline. You need to be aware that people are driven by feelings, generally away from pain and towards pleasure. To translate the science of feelings to the classroom, your students want to feel good. That doesn't mean you have to massage their egos and offer insincere praise, it merely suggests you have to create an environment where students feel wanted, respected, valued. We're not saying it's easy. And there are probably some students who, deep down, you don't think are worth respecting and valuing... but stick with this chapter and we'll hope to change your mind.

> *Pretend that every single person you meet has a sign around his or her neck that says, 'Make Me Feel Important'. Not only will you succeed in sales, you will succeed in life.*
>
> **Mary Kay Ash**

It is worth saying at this point that when you move on from your first school to a second school, you will have to start all over again! You may have been the most respected member of staff at your last school, but your new pupils won't know that. At least not straight away. I remember arriving at my third school as head of department, feeling as though I should know a thing or two and being quite non-plussed by kids being rude, cheeky and awkward. I had to start from scratch, like everyone else.[46]

So... discipline! We've included this chapter late on in the book because everything we've written

---

[46] But please don't use this as an excuse to stay in one school for forty years!

before is part of you 'getting your discipline'. So, all the previous tricks of the trade apply.

Knowing me, knowing you, Aha!

You will start to build your discipline as soon as you start building relationships with the pupils you teach, and it is always worthwhile starting with the particularly challenging ones. Your best way of maintaining discipline is to create rapport. And one of the easiest ways to do this is to learn their names. There is nothing worse than trying to control a new class in a new school environment when you are saying, 'You, will you turn round, please! No, not you, (pointing) you!'

'What, me Miss, I wasn't even doing anything!'

'I know you weren't doing anything. I'm not pointing at you, I'm looking at the girl with blond hair behind you!'

'Me, I never said a word!'

'Not YOU, YOUUU!' and so it goes on. Nightmare!

Very important then. Learn their names as soon as possible and set yourself targets: 'I am going to learn five more today!' And check them off in your register or mark book.

However, I would go one further than that. Not only should you learn their names, but learn two things about each one of them and be quite methodical about it. Set yourself a target for each break time to engage at least two in purposeful conversation. When you start to know who has got a new puppy, who has got a birthday, who plays netball, who has a brother/sister, who likes Heavy Metal and so on, you have got the necessary starting ammunition to start to build your relationships.

This paves the way for what we call mini-conversations, which will be the extra spice in how you create relationships in and out of the classroom.

Again, you must be quite methodical about this. Make a note in your mark book when you have found out your two things for each child, so that you can be sure you haven't missed anyone out. This will allow you to have mini-conversations whenever you meet these kids out and about. As kids come into the classroom for the next lesson, it works wonders if you can greet them with a private but cheery word of welcome, along the lines of, 'How's that puppy?' 'Did you score in the match at the weekend?' or 'Thought of you on Sunday when I saw that programme about X on the TV.' These mini-conversations are the start of your discipline. It doesn't take much, but by showing you care or are interested in their lives beyond the classroom, you begin to create a bond.

Seating plans

Yes, seating plans! Nothing will communicate the fact that Sir or Miss knows what they are doing and that they are in control better than a seating plan. I have heard discussions through the years about whether the teacher should impose their will on the class in this way. Remember the law of the jungle: someone will seize control of your classroom. Now, it's either you or it's them, and if it's them, I am prepared to bet it won't be the compliant, polite and hard-working pupils. I am unequivocal about this, you set the tone and that means you tell them where to sit. It sends a massively important subconscious message that you are in charge.

I usually get the pupils in and sit them down, saying, 'Don't get anything out. You are about to move!' I have previously drawn a map of the tables in the room and allocated children to tables. I then go round the room, map in hand, pointing to each place saying who is going to sit there, and I say to them, 'When I have finished talking, you move!' This way you can re-seat a class in under a minute, guaranteed.

What are your choices? Let's look at a few possibilities.

1. Alphabetical? The advantages? It is uncontroversial and clear-cut. To the kid who says, 'Oh, why do I have to sit next to him?' the answer is non-negotiable. It is a good way, probably, of splitting up the troublemakers, unless their names happen to be sequential in the alphabet! And remember what we said about using kids' names, both for seating plans and when you are calling the register - start with the Ws or go alternately top and bottom. They will love you for it, and Andrew Adams may like not always being first up as well!

2. Boy/Girl. With older pupils you will almost certainly endure one minute and thirteen seconds (roughly) of chuntering and then they will get on with it and you will have a much better lesson.[47]

3. Friends. I tend to avoid this because I know what I would have done if I had sat with my friends at school - chat and not concentrate!

---

[47] Many teachers go with the easy option of letting pupils sit with whomever they want. We firmly believe that part of gaining discipline is endure seventy-three seconds of hassle. It pays you back a million times over during the school year.

I am very hesitant about friends working together, but there may be times when you judge it to be desirable.

4. If you are working in a primary school environment, you may want to consider ability groupings, so that each table is either composed of children of similar abilities or you actually want deliberately to have a mix of abilities.

How often should you change your seating plan? We feel that ideally you should change your seating plan three times a term. Whatever you feel about this, one thing is for sure, changing your seating plan is a brilliant way of refreshing your classroom. Maybe it has been a long session; try changing the seating plan for the last half hour. There are various ways you can achieve this: you could go round the class labelling children as Oranges and Lemons (little kids), Ferraris and BMWs (early secondary) or beer and wine (older kids), and then you get one category to stand up and you instruct them to sit next to a different person they have not sat with before.

I would suggest the end of November as a really good time to re-seat your classes. They are beginning to get restless and tired. Christmas is still a long way off. You are also probably getting tired and restless, so have a new seating arrangement. Maybe even change the table formation in the room. Go from rows to groups or individual tables. It is amazing how this can rejuvenate a classroom. Try it and see!

Do use your seating plan as an instrument of 'divide and rule', particularly when you have some awkward customers! Cast them to the four corners of your room, preferably out of eye-line with each other.[48] Equally, do not be anxious about leaving spare seats. There are some children who have wall-to-wall problems with the rest of the human race so, fine, sit them on their own if you have the space to do so. And do not shirk the issue if they challenge you about it. Say to them, 'You are sitting there because you work better on your own, and I want you to do as well as possible in this lesson.'

If you are doubting any of this, I'd draw your attention back to the fact that, subconsciously, children expect you to control them. They have a preconceived notion that school is about learning and the teacher should be in control. So, while some will challenge your authority, you need to stand firm (but fair). Your consistent message, both consciously and unconsciously, sends an unmistakable message to your pupils that this is your classroom and *you* are in control. That is where discipline starts.

Resilience

> *It is impossible to live without failing at something, unless you live so cautiously that you might as well not have lived at all - in which case, you fail by default.*
>
> **JK Rowling**

In the fantastic novel, A Kestrel for a Knave, there's a brilliant scene which all teachers can learn

---

[48] I know, I know, I hear you say that with your class from hell you would need twenty-eight corners. Unfortunately classrooms aren't built like that, but you get the point.

from. In fact, every teacher should read the book and, indeed, watch the equally fantastic movie version, Kes, as there's so much there that's useful for a developing teacher, both in what to do and specifically what not to do. For the moment, though, I want to concentrate on how the headteacher, Mr Gryce (or 'Gryce Pudding' to his pupils) deals with a group of boys who have been caught smoking. The group, unknown to Gryce, has been joined by another pupil sent by a teacher with a message for the head. Gryce takes the group into his office and proceeds to rant at them about their lack of decency, manners or morals while ignoring every effort the young lad with a message makes to deliver it. He attacks the important things in their life, their 'gear' and their 'music', and accuses them of not listening to his repeated warnings (which is ironic as he is not listening to the messenger). Gryce goes on to use his solution to their crimes and brutally canes all of the boys, including the unfortunate messenger.

What can we learn from this, then? In every survey I have ever done with pupils, the biggest gripe they have is about teachers who do not listen to them.

> *Enough about me. Now let's talk about you. Tell me, what do you think about me?*
>
> **Anonymous**

Mr Gryce caned an innocent boy who, in real life, would bear that scar forever. I am going to suggest to you that in your career you will occasionally get it wrong in the same manner though not, I hope, in such a violent manner. It's so easy to get it wrong in the heat of the moment, when there's a distraction on the table where the 'class clown' sits. The danger is that you assume the clown is yet again responsible for the disruption of the lesson. Be sure you are right, and if you're not, deal with the issue without apportioning blame and use your classroom management skills to avoid any further problems. Get it wrong and you'll begin to create a pupil with a grudge who is less likely to work for you.

Similarly, it would certainly be a rare occasion if every single pupil in a class behaved badly, yet far too often I hear whole classes labelled as being difficult or having been particularly challenging. Worse still, I have come across occasions where the whole class has been punished. This means that those pupils who were not responsible for any difficulties were punished for the misdemeanours of others. This is no way to build positive relationships. More often than not, when I have had cause to examine the reasons for such problems, it has typically been poor classroom management or unsuitable work set for a cover teacher that has led to things going wrong.

Think back to the first part of this book. Ginott makes it clear that teachers choose whether to humanise or de-humanise their pupils. Mr Gryce at no point shows his pupils that there is another way to behave, and his beating simply undermines their already tenuous appreciation of the education system and does nothing to help them learn a different way of behaving. In disrespecting the things they like he does not identify with the 'kid culture' of the time and, because of this, he makes no connection with them. You can't imagine Mr Gryce having meaningful mini-conversations or using praise as a motivational tool.

Getting it wrong

> *In business, when things aren't working it's time to mix it up.*
>
> **Donald Trump**

Another classic means of getting it wrong is missing kids getting it right! Do that at your peril as the light-bulb moments are the key points when you need to grab hold of the reins and lead the learning. A basic rule of teaching, whatever the age of the pupils, is to catch students doing things well and tell them. So, if someone gives you a fantastic answer or tries exceptionally hard or is focused for the whole lesson or helps another pupil (etc.), either praise them there and then or, alternatively, pull them to one side on the way out of the lesson. 'James, I'd like to thank you for your brilliant behaviour today. Absolutely fantastic. It was a real help to me and you've contributed to making this a fantastic lesson.' It'll take you ten seconds. The simple truth is that James will want to repeat that behaviour.

Please note, I am not advocating false praise or that you go overboard, merely that you make a point of catching people doing things well and tell them. As a teacher you lead the learning in the classroom and, just like great leaders in history, you need to seize the moment and deploy all of your skills to make it really count.[49]

You will make mistakes; learn from them, learn from the mistakes you will see your colleagues make

---

[49] Please feel free to apply the same principles to colleagues who handle things well. Notice it and tell them!

and aim to not repeat them. Manage that and your pupils will rate you and follow you.

It's the effort that counts!

While we are talking about praise, let's share some fascinating research by Carol Dweck, a professor at Stanford University. The research also features in Matthew Syed's book Bounce, in which Syed, who is one of the UK's finest table-tennis players, explores the factors which contributed to his phenomenal success. His startling conclusion is that he had no genetic predisposition towards being a gifted player. Instead, his skill was derived from the influence exerted on him by various people who had a huge bearing on his development. Plus 10,000 hours of practice!

> *You miss 100% of the shots you never take.*
>
> **Wayne Gretsky, hockey star**

So, if you are intrigued by the eternal 'nurture versus nature' debate, here is our take on Carol Dweck's work.

Dweck spent hours of research exploring the factors which influence the development of talent. She agrees that there are two schools of thought or 'mindsets': on the one hand are those who think talent is down to innate, God-given ability (closely akin to the 'nature' side of the argument) and on the other those who think talent is developed through effort and deliberate hard work (tied in with the 'nurture' school of thought).

Dweck's research is directly relevant to the teaching profession because she conducted research with

400 eleven year olds in which she set them a series of puzzles to solve. At the end of the exercise she gave them their scores and six words of praise. Half were given praise which suggested that they were gifted and intelligent at solving puzzles, such as, 'You are smart at this.' The other half were given praise reflecting the effort they had put in, such as, 'You must have worked really hard.' She then gave them the choice of attempting a test of similar difficulty or a much harder test, and the results were startling. Those who were praised for their intelligence were markedly less willing to take on the tougher challenge, as if they were frightened of 'failing' and therefore losing their 'smart' status. Those who were given effort-based praise were much more up for the challenge.

Then she took it a stage further and gave all the children a very tough test. None of them did very well, but those who had been given praise based on their intelligence were completely de-motivated, as though this proved that actually they weren't very good after all. Those who were given effort-based praise really got their teeth into the exercise. They achieved more and stayed at the task much longer.

Dweck distinguishes between what she calls a 'fixed mindset' and a 'growth mindset', born out in the final test. She then gave the children a test of equal difficulty to the first one: those who were praised for their intelligence showed a noticeable drop in their results, whereas those who were praised for effort increased their score by 30%. Dweck has repeated this research several times in different contexts but with identical results.

This alludes to the power of words. Dweck is emphatic in her conclusion that praising children's intelligence harms their motivation and their overall performance, whereas praise that reflects their *effort* stimulates performance by creating a growth mindset.

So teachers who want to engage should equip themselves with the kind of feedback below:

- 'You've really worked hard at that, and that is why it has turned out so well.'

- 'Great effort! You are much further along the road to...'

- 'Top effort! Now you are in business!'

- 'That's the best result you have achieved in this topic so far. Now, if we can work really hard at ..., you will be able to...'

- 'At the beginning of the week, none of you were any good at this, because we hadn't done it before. But now, with all the work we have put into it, look where we have got to! And next...'

Try it! You will be amazed how it can help to stretch your most able performers, but also how it throws a lifeline of hope to those who had written themselves off as no-hopers.

It also works outside of the classroom. After years of resistance I have recently joined a gym. I was dreading my first appointment with my personal trainer, faced with a bewildering array of athletic equipment most of which I reckoned I had last seen in a medieval torture chamber. I must be the most unnatural athlete he has ever encountered, but as we explored the possibilities of various machines with intimidating blocks of weights ready to threaten my musculature, he took me through a range of exercises and his praise was constant: 'Top effort! Well done!' he purred as I struggled against the constraints of gravity. I came away under no illusion that I was suddenly ready to take on a marathon, but I felt rewarded for my efforts, keen to come back the next day and determined to improve my scores. Result!

The Matthew Effect

And, before we finish this chapter, allow us to introduce something that is thought provoking at the very least. The 'Matthew Effect' is a rule of life. It describes a situation in which an initial success in something leads to even greater success. And, conversely, if we are *unsuccessful*, we're likely to become even more unsuccessful. In short, it seems that success and failure will grow like Topsy, whichever gets the upper hand. The effect derives its name from a passage in the Gospel of St Matthew, 25:29 *To everyone who has, will more be given, and he will have abundance. But from him who has not, even what he has will be taken away.*

Heavy stuff. But most probably true. Let me give you a school example: children who start off reading well will get better and better compared with their peers, because they will read even more broadly and quickly. The more words they learn the easier and more enjoyable it becomes. The get hooked and they're off. On the other hand, it's very hard for poor readers to catch up because, for them, the spiral goes downwards. Due to the Matthew Effect, the gap between those who read well and those who read poorly grows even bigger rather than smaller

That's the 'Matthew Effect': success snowballs, but so does failure. The rich get richer and the poor poorer. This means it's vital to get our spiral going in the right direction, preferably at an early age.

Poor behaviour is also a Matthew phenomenon. Unruly behaviour at an early age means the child will be chastised often. They will quickly grow to hate school and their sullen attitude is a barrier to learning. So, guess what? They fall behind, which exacerbates the problem and their negative attitudes harden. By the time they get to 'big school' they may well be learning phobic. They skip lessons and when they do turn up it's because they are legally obliged to. Tough kids for sure. But, hey, cut them some slack, society's made them that way!

How does it relate to your classroom and discipline? Set the children up for some early successes. Boost their confidence in your subject. If they 'get it' early on, the spiral of learning looks after itself.

Top tips

1. Be consistent. Be fair.

2. Get to know names, hobbies, interests, etc. Create rapport.

3. Have a seating plan. Change it termly.

4. Catch pupils doing things well and tell them.

5. Be aware of The Matthew Effect. Create a few quick wins.

Bonus story

Yes, yes, it's an oldie. And it's a bit smulchy. But we like it, so here goes:

Early one morning a British tourist woke up and stepped out onto his balcony. He breathed in the warm air. Brazil. Mmmm. Copa Cabaña Beach. The ocean pounding against miles and miles of deserted golden sand. No wonder, it was 5 a.m.! He rubbed the sleep from his eyes and set off to dip his toes into the froth. As he stepped onto the beach he saw there was one other person on the beach, standing at the water's edge. He was throwing things into the sea. The tourist was curious so he approached the fellow. He watched as the man bent down, picked up a tiny starfish and threw it into the sea. Plop. Then another. And another. The tourist noticed that the beach was covered in *millions* of these starfish, presumably washed up at high tide. He approached the stranger and asked him what he was doing.

'I'm rescuing the starfish,' shouted the man above the roar of the ocean. 'They've been washed up. They need to get back into the sea otherwise they will dry out. Or even worse,' he said, pointing to the circling birds, 'the gulls will eat them.'

The tourist looked left. Three miles of beach stretched into the distance. And right, three miles more. 'But it's hopeless,' he said. 'There are millions of starfish! What difference can you make?'

The local bent down and picked up a starfish from the sand. He tossed it into the ocean. *Plop*. 'I made a difference to that one.'[50]

---

[50] Based on a story in *Chicken Soup for the Soul*, Canfield & Hansen.

Chapter 11

The class from hell

'Supposing a tree fell down, Pooh, when we were underneath it?'

'Supposing it didn't,' said Pooh after careful thought.

Piglet was comforted by this.

A. A. Milne

In a nutshell

The final piece of our 'discipline two-parter' starts with a bit of perspective. We take a look at the big wide world and acknowledge that, yes, there are some challenging kids out there. Society has a lot to answer for! So, chill a bit. We focus on some strategies that you can use on the 'nutters'.[51] We remind you of the importance of keeping cool under pressure and how best to manage your classroom when things go pear shaped. We chuck in a few acronyms (SEAL, EQ, NLP) and introduce the concept of 'perceptual positioning'. We examine the use of positive language and give plenty of real-world examples. We share some great strategies for dealing with foul language

---

[51] No apologies for the un-pc reference. I once worked in a school and the head addressed a hand-selected group of notoriously difficult boys with 'Good morning, nutters.' I looked shocked. The 'nutters' loved it!

(the pupils', not yours!) as well as detentions and student contracts. Winnie the Pooh contributes two final quotes and we end with a block-busting story about Buddha. *What a finish!*

An imperfect world

Doing the business with difficult classes and difficult kids - this is probably the biggest challenge faced by many teachers! Unruly pupils used to be the preserve of a few classes from Year 9 upwards, but anecdotal evidence suggests that it's spreading. We hear of primary school children throwing major tantrums, and violence against teachers is on the rise.

All three of your authors admit to having terrible days, beaten into submission by the children of Beelzebub.

In the real world, there are parts of the country where children don't get anywhere near adequate parenting. The 'Matthew Effect' has been spiralling them downwards since they came out of the womb!

You will have horror stories of your own, so there is no value in us stating the obvious. Put simply, some children have no boundaries, they see no value in education and they have no positive role models at home. And, yes, even through our optimistic positive psychology goggles, these pupils will be challenging. Some schools are set in the middle of low aspiration communities where challenging behaviours have been passed down through the generations. Fact!

Yet herein lies one of the most knee-shakingly exciting challenges of the teaching profession. How many of these children can we engage, either in learning or in some semblance of positive conversation? Remember, you could be the only positive person in their life. So our first plea is, as tempting and easy as it may be, don't give up on these children. Sure, they can (and will) drive you to despair. But, if you get it right, your results with these children will also be your greatest triumphs.

We've all engaged challenging individuals. But what about when they accumulate in 'the class from hell'? We have all taught them, haven't we? The class that you dread, time after time after time. One of my colleagues used to refer to '4M days', in other words days, when she had to face the infamous class 4M. These classes will haunt our dreams for the rest of time and the individual characters will stay with us until our dying day!

There is possibly nothing worse in our chosen profession than that feeling that a class has got the better of you, you have lost control of them and they have run rings round you. It is intensely hurtful to your pride and self-esteem, as well as being an incredibly exhausting experience that leaves you feeling absolutely drained afterwards, so clearly it merits some major attention in this book.

Get a proper perspective

> *You can put your boots in the oven but that don't make them biscuits.*
>
> **Dallas DJ, 103.3FM**

First, we need to get things in perspective. 'They only play up for me!' and 'They were horrendous today!' These are two of the most common comments I have heard in the aftermath of a lesson that has not gone well. 'It's only me?' I wonder how far you have to go along your professional journey before you start to hear the names of those who have plagued you with their bad behaviour and their rudeness mentioned in the course of staffroom dialogue. Almost certainly these villains of the peace will not be selecting you for any special preferential treatment. Almost certainly they will be known faces and your lesson is not, therefore, an isolated incident. There is nothing worse than allowing yourself to harbour the suspicion that these little fiends are in fact angels for everyone else.

The next thing we need to think about is what we said at the start of this book. Most of the pupils we have met have been great to work with and it is only a minority that unfortunately stand out for all the wrong reasons. That means, in writing this section, we are very aware of a number of things:

- The class from hell is defined in the context of your experience and the other classes you have taught. You will naturally have classes you enjoy more than others, and for all sorts of reasons.

- Your experience with that class will be part of your learning experience and that same class, if you could have them all over again in say five years' time, would probably not be as challenging.

- There are ways and means of turning that class into a personal achievement.

So what about, 'they were horrendous today'? Remember the brief introduction to generalising and distorting from Chapter 5? Whenever I have been helping a colleague who has let off steam after a difficult lesson, I have made them press their pause button and asked them, 'What all of them, for the whole duration of the lesson?' Immediately my colleague tends to backtrack, along these lines: 'Well, no, not all of them. The boys in the middle desks were fine, and actually the girls in the back corner were OK,' and 'Actually, they weren't too bad at the beginning, and they did that task quite well. It was when I got to the writing that it all went wrong!'

Resilience

It's worth diverting off for a brief reminder about resilience. If you want to aspire to being an average teacher then all you have to do is replicate what everyone around you is doing. Being a super-teacher requires you to have a wow factor and to take a few risks. It means you might have to be a bit edgy in how and what you teach. And sometimes, things will fail. Sometimes, the hardcore 4Ms might get the better of you. But, in true super-teacher fashion, that doesn't stop you from being creative. You tweak things for next time and in good old-fashioned personal development language, you take the learning and move forward.

Bouncebackability is one of Andy's points from earlier in the book. What compounds the discipline situation is that bouncebackability is the hardest of the points to achieve!

Please don't get caught in catastrophising. Beware! Your brain is expert at what psychologists call 'deficiency focusing' or 'awfulising'.

'It's snowing still,' said Eeyore gloomily.

'So it is.'

'And freezing.'

'Is it?'

'Yes,' said Eeyore. 'However,' he said, brightening up a little, 'we haven't had an earthquake lately.'

A. A. Milne

There's always a bright side... sometimes it's not obvious, but it's there if you get in the habit of looking in the right place.

Here's a reminder of the questions taken from Paul McGee's superb SUMO[52] book. Use them when things don't go so well. By asking yourself the right questions you are much less likely to beat yourself up when things go wrong. In fact, these questions will help you remain upbeat and resourceful enough to move forward:

1. Where is this issue on a scale of 1 to 10?

2. How important will this be in six months' time?

3. Is my response appropriate and effective?

4. How can I influence or improve the situation?

5. How can I learn from this?

6. What will I do differently next time?

7. What can I find that's positive in this situation?

> *Never become irritable waiting for things to get better. If you'll be patient, you'll find that you can wait much faster.*
>
> **Unknown**

The 'nutters'

Your first objective must be to work out in your mind which members of the class you can get in your pocket. Remember what we have said about mini-conversations and finding out things about your kids? Conversations in which you show that you have remembered that they are into rap, or they have a younger sister whom you teach, or

---

[52] SUMO stands for 'shut up and move on' and is well worth a read.

their birthday is next week? Remembering these little beauties will be worth their weight in gold to you. Don't forget to be completely methodical about this, by which I mean make a note in your mark book of whom you are targeting and when you have seen them. Otherwise it won't happen. These are now your bankers who are least likely to play you up next time. Work your way through the whole class as quickly as possible, heading for your kingpins, the ringleaders. These might seem like tough nuts, but they are definitely crackable. In psychobabble speak we call them 'rapport leaders'. In terms of classroom strategy it means if you can get them on board they will influence those around them.

4M were known as 'The class from Hell'.

It may well be that you need help to deal with these. Teachers are very proud animals and we often don't like to admit that we are having problems. At the beginning of your career, do not be ashamed to be a magpie. Steal from other people. Borrow ideas from more experienced colleagues. Work out strategies with them. This could be your head of department or a colleague next door. It might take the form of agreeing to send someone who is uncooperative to them if they play you up again. If you suspect that they won't go, then use the unmarked brown envelope trick. Have an unmarked brown envelope on your desk and, if you want to move a particular pupil, send a reliable pupil next door with the envelope for your colleague with whom you have a pre-arranged agreement, who will recognise this as an SOS and will come and calmly take out whoever it might be who is giving you grief. Indeed, you can send the person you want to move to your colleague's room with a message in a sealed envelope. Make your arrangements and be prepared to reciprocate too.

With a class like this it is absolutely essential that all the things we talked about in terms of classroom management are razor sharp. These kids will only need a microsecond to turn the lesson to their advantage, and they will pounce mercilessly on any evidence of poor organisation on your part. Think about what we said earlier about being at your door as they come in. Your most powerful weapon is your eyes. Use them to establish positive eye contact with each of the hard nuts as they come through the door. Greet them with a comment that starts the lesson on a positive note. 'Good to see you. We've got a really good lesson lined up for you today.' or 'Good to see you. When you had your mind to it, you impressed me on

Tuesday. I think there is more to you than meets the eye.' 'Damien, you're going to like this today and I've got a special section in the lesson I know you'll enjoy.' (Because you've done your homework you know Damien's into motorbikes and you've incorporated this into the lesson.)

Do think about the seating or grouping arrangements. Remember the divide and rule theory, and be quite insistent about it. They may well say, 'I don't want to...' to which I always say, 'I didn't want to get out of bed this morning. There are loads of things I don't want to do, but I have to do them. So do you.' Never forget the fundamental demands the kids make of you; that you control them and that you teach them something. This is about control! You decide who they will work with, which means you are in control.

Here's something that's worth thinking about. If there is one pupil who particularly plagues you, it is often worth a little scan round the playground to see if you can spot them before the lesson even starts. Of course check your findings with the office, but if you do find that they are away, it does wonders for your confidence as the nightmare hour approaches! If you do spot them, see if you can bump into them deliberately for a mini-conversation first. Fortune favours the brave!

Doing a runner!

(No, not you. Them!)

What happens if, despite all your best efforts, a pupil either takes you on or does a runner? If one tries to square up to you, walk away with words like, 'I am not going to discuss this with you now,' and if possible sit down. It is much harder for them to go toe-to-toe with you if you are seated. Always buy time, rather than take the matter on while your heart is pumping and the situation is providing grandstand entertainment for all the others. You will almost certainly need to get help at this point and this is where your brown envelope may come in useful. If they run out of the classroom, let them go! Don't try to restrain them physically because you may end up having to justify yourself when actually they were wholly in the wrong. Let them go. I always say, quite calmly, 'If you want to go, go. We will all still be here tomorrow and we will sort it out then.' Then inform the office as soon as possible that the child has left your room. Your senior leadership team are paid more money than you for a reason - their job is supposed to be harder. So, you can stay calm and teach the rest of the class while they sort it out.

Please do not feel guilty or bad about passing miscreants up the hierarchy. Your responsibility lies with teaching the ones who are in your classroom. Often, the other kids will feel a sense of relief that the trouble-causer has been moved on and, if you remain calm and in control, there will be an undercurrent of wow!

Sock it to 'em

The key to the whole lesson is the start. Think about all those things we said to think about before the first child appears. Be a model of confidence and positivity. Think about your body language. Stand like a 2%er. Smile![53]

---

[53] Yes, it might be fake! But your physiology and psychology are connected. If you smile, your brain immediately pumps out positive chemicals and good feelings will follow. No, of course we're not advocating inanely grinning at pupils for no reason! Just some thought as to your general demeanour. Confidence and positivity are contagious!

Have something for them to do as soon as they arrive. Either have something on the screen, or have some music playing or a DVD playing something relevant, or have something on their desks for them to do. Now that YouTube has arrived, there is very little excuse for not being able to find something which will broadcast on Radio WiiFM to engage their attention. The Devil always makes work for idle hands, so get them busy as soon as possible. Think of things that you know they can do and hopefully actually like doing. Exercises involving prioritising, putting things in order, matching or finding an odd one out are always good starters, especially where there is no one right or wrong answer, so they have a chance to start a lesson by getting something right. You are starting with a feel-good factor. Remember the Matthew Effect? Success breeds success!

That sinking feeling

How can they say my life is not a success? Have I not for more than sixty years got enough to eat and escaped being eaten?

Logan P. Smith

But what if it is still going horribly wrong? As you feel yourself getting het up, your obvious reaction is to want to scream and shout. When your voice is measured and controlled, there is nothing wrong with raising it to impose yourself upon the class, to cut through all the rubbish that they are throwing your way so that the natural habitat for learning can be restored. In fact, most of the class will be willing you to restore order. They much prefer it when you are in control to when the loud-mouthed and ignorant take charge. There is a shallow pleasure in messing about, but the real feel-good factor only comes from a lesson in which everyone has worked hard and achieved something in an atmosphere that is calm and orderly.

However, there is a world of difference between positively challenging an unruly minority and an uncontrolled screaming match, the rant in which you vent all your innermost frustrations. We've seen and heard it and it never works. The ranter starts with one of the miscreants and typically works their way through all their manifest shortcomings, taking a side swipe at their siblings, who no doubt were just as bad, if not worse, then moving on to someone else, adding in their crimes from last week as well just for good measure! Not good for your blood pressure or respect from other pupils.

Emotional intelligence

SEAL has become an important area of thinking, recently, for the relationships teachers seek to establish with those they teach. SEAL: social and emotional aspects of learning. In a nutshell, you are much more likely to establish appropriate relationships with your pupils if you avoid the sort of cutting slanging matches outlined above. A very challenging boy once said to me, 'I hate it when teachers shout. It means they don't care.' I am not sure I agree with him, but it was his perception. He was a very challenging pupil who will have driven teacher after teacher to distraction with his poor behaviour, but nonetheless he is suggesting that the teachers he did get on with were those who didn't shout and scream.

> '*Piglet*', *said Rabbit, taking out a pencil and licking the end of it,* '*you haven't any pluck.*'
>
> '*It is hard to be brave,*' *said Piglet, sniffling slightly,* '*when you're only a Very Small Animal.*'
>
> **A. A. Milne**

Here's an interesting activity. It requires you to be alone in your classroom, so early morning or last thing are best. Go and sit in a 'problem pupil's' chair and look towards the front of the classroom. Imagine what he or she sees. What do you look like from the student's point of view? What is your body language? Does she or he see you smiling and confident or stern and foreboding? And, from the problem pupil's perspective, listen to yourself. What does this pupil hear you saying? The words? The tone of voice? Confident and controlled or hesitant, shrieking and desperate? And, experiencing it entirely from the perspective of the problem pupil, how do you feel? Put yourself, as far as you dare, into their mindset. What feelings and emotions do they have while they sit in your class?

Now you have a bit more information - very useful information - because it comes from a perspective that we don't usually experience. The big question is, 'Now I've experienced my lesson from their perspective, what can I do to improve the relationship?'

Stay with me! I appreciate this may seem harsh. You might well be asking yourself, doesn't the pupil have to change? You might be screaming at this book, 'It's not me... it's them!' The chances are you cannot change the pupil. At least not in terms of forcing them to engage in your lesson. But you can influence them. Massively! And this is the key. This different perspective will trigger some ways that you can behave that will build rapport. In neurolinguistic programming they call this activity 'perceptual positioning' and I've found it useful on a number of occasions to help me modify *my* behaviour in order to create a better relationship.

Positive language

> *They can because they think they can.*[54]
>
> **Virgil**

Here are some ways of dealing with some of your most awkward customers that may help. These are especially useful when you are speaking privately to a pupil who has given you particular grief.

I often start by saying something like, 'Emma, you are a massively capable person.' I may even qualify that by saying things like, 'You are sharp, you are quick, you get on well with people... I like you. You've got a good smile. You've got something about you.' This is quite a good code which will be readily understood as meaning, 'You are not always the easiest to get along with, but you are an okay person.' Always start with something positive, then work towards what the problem is and be quite specific: 'There is a difficulty and that is...'. Remember that this is the Y generation so it can help if you explain why this issue must be addressed. Explanations like, 'If you carry on your own conversation, you really annoy the other kids

---

[54] Err, no, not that one!

because they can't listen and concentrate.' Don't pull any punches either. It is perfectly in order to say, 'Just to carry on and do what you want all the time would be regarded in the big outside world as just plain rude and selfish!'

I will often preface what I am going to say with, 'I wouldn't be much of a teacher if I just shrugged my shoulders and said, "Oh well, it doesn't matter!" I would be letting you grow up thinking it was okay to... '.

So the next part of the conversation could be like this: 'If you do that when you are a grown up, you will find yourself at a huge disadvantage.' Then go on to say, 'If you do that when you go out to work, you will get one warning, and then you will be sacked. I have got a lot of time for you and I don't want to see that happen to you. I am not going to give up on you. I want to see you do well.'

However, here's another way. Ask the pupil what they see themselves doing in ten to fifteen years' time. Then ask them what they think their boss would think about them if they chose to behave in the way they had done with you. Follow this by asking what the outcome might be. This then leads on to a discussion about owning the outcomes of personal behaviour. This means the pupil is coming up with the answers, not you.

Another tack I have used very effectively is to say, 'I have no idea what job you are going to do when you are older, but whatever you decide upon, it is a priceless gift to be able to walk into a room, any room, and get on with the people in that room, and for them to get on with you. Now today, you weren't able to meet that challenge. You weren't able to get on with the person in charge, that is me as your teacher, and you irritated other kids in the room because you made it difficult for them to learn.' Possibly, depending on how confident you're feeling, follow up with, 'So what can you do differently to create a better impression?'

During the class it is always effective to empower the pupil to find a solution that will work. If someone is misbehaving, go up to them quite calmly and say, 'I can't have you doing that. You will annoy everyone else in the room. You have two choices. Either you do the right thing from now until the end of the lesson or you will have to go and work with Mrs... Which are you going to do?' And get them to commit by saying, 'I am going to behave.' If they err again you can remind them of this. You have got a hook to work with.

It is always useful to think through how to respond to the old chestnut, 'It's boring. I don't see the point in learning.' I again refer back to the world of work and say, 'You may not need to know anything about quadrilateral equations but what you will need to do is stick with it, even when it is boring. You will have to do what you are asked to by the person in charge, get on with the other people you work with, etc.' This way I am leading them to see that school is like a dress rehearsal for life. From the age of four to eighteen they will try their hand at all kinds of different things like maths, English, science, a foreign language, music, PE and so on. Some they will like, some they won't; some they will see the point of, some they won't; but day in, day out they are learning the skills they will need to do well in whatever job they choose to pursue, e.g. being on time, presenting things on paper effectively, cooperating with other people, being well turned out, doing as they are asked, even when they don't want to do whatever it is. I have found this to be an extremely effective way of separating the content of a particular part of the curriculum from the skills they are learning as a by-product, which will be indispensable to them as they grow up.

Rules of the road

Here are some more tactics for talking to very difficult and probably older pupils. Have an old copy of a roadmap and say, 'We have got a problem here. If you were driving me as your passenger from here to here (pointing at two towns on the map), I feel like the map-reader who says, "At this roundabout, turn this way", but you say, "Nah, I'm going to go my own way!" Your teachers are showing the right way and yet time after time, you don't take any notice, and the result is that you won't reach the destination you want!' Very effective.

You can alter this to ask them to show you on the map how you get from where you are to a chosen place further afield. They typically will follow a reasonably direct route with their finger. Ask them why they didn't go via some out-of-the-way place, which can then lead into a discussion about choosing the right paths to get to an ultimate life goal.

Another is the spoof job advert that specifies the qualities wanted for a particular mythical job, but one that this pupil might be interested in. Something along the lines of 'Assistant Security Officer' at the local out of town shopping complex or 'Sales Receptionist' at a local garden centre. The kid will probably challenge you by saying, 'Is this real?' Call their bluff and say yes! Include details of the salary, something along the lines of 'Above minimum wage' will do. In your spoof advert list the qualities required for the job, e.g. good school record, gets on well with people, always respects the person in charge, punctual, etc. (including the behaviour which is causing you grief). Invite the pupil to look down the list and say whether they would be qualified. Explain to them why, if you were the boss, you would need to be persuaded that they were the ideal candidate. Obviously you will want to zoom in on the area where they are clearly nowhere near a position where they would stand a chance of getting this type of job.

I am suggesting these strategies to you as a means of engaging these hard-to-reach kids who are disrupting your lesson in a way which does not involve 'in your face' shouting and screaming, which you might feel like doing from time to time, but which will almost always backfire. In the worst-case scenario the pupil goes home and complains, probably with their own version of the story, and you end up on the defensive towards an aggressive parent with a doubly awkward kid.

The whole SEAL initiative has forced a rethink about how we deal with pupils in such a way that they don't resent sanctimonious teachers. Even more than that, it's back to Ginott and the idea of humanising your pupils, helping them to see that there are other ways to get the most out of life. That is a Holy Grail for most teachers. The opposite is more likely to result in them continuing to be even more difficult and, if that teacher teaches in one school long enough, they may well find that their old antagonists instil the same values in their offspring when they come along.

Crying foul

Children see Premiership footballers abusing referees every game. Foul language has become common parlance, even in some very young children, but it needn't be in your classroom.[55] If they use foul language in my lesson or in my hearing, I always get them to write down the words they used. I take it to the school office and ask one of the secretaries to photocopy what they have written three times. When I return, I put each one on the desk in front of them and say, 'If I hear you use language like that again, I will put one copy on the headteacher's desk, one in your school file and I shall send one to your family. Will I need to do that?' Usually the answer is a very solemn, 'No!'

Another useful tactic is the pre-written letter to their family, already typed on school headed paper, which details, for the benefit of their family, exactly what they have done wrong. I sit them down and read it to them and then say, 'If you repeat that kind of behaviour, I will send this letter home. Will I need to send it?' You might, of course, think that it should be sent straight away, and maybe this is true for some behaviour. However, there are many ways to skin a cat and there's nothing wrong with trying a bit of leverage first.

Think carefully about sending kids out. There is nothing worse than sending out a troublemaker

---

[55] I cannot *not* share this one! Doing a talk in a primary school I asked, 'Who's got a pet?' I chose one hand from the forest. 'What have you got?'
'A parrot sir,' beamed the six year old.
'Excellent. And does it talk?'
The teachers were shaking their heads in a 'Don't go there' kind of way, but it was too late. 'Yes sir,' replied the child. 'My dad throws a blanket over it to catch it and it shouts "F**k off!" '

who has been an absolute thorn in your side, only to find that he or she is out in the corridor pulling faces at the other kids or constantly coming to your door to continue the disruption with an endless succession of plausible excuses along the lines of, 'Can I go to the toilet? Can I come back in?' etc. Mostly, it's best to send someone out for only a short period to make a point or to diffuse an escalating problem. If you think they need longer, it is much more effective if you are prepared and can send him or her either to a colleague or to sit at a pre-arranged quiet table with idiot-proof work for them to do. It is a greater deterrent and will cause you much less hassle.

Detention

A brief word about detentions. First and foremost, do find out what your school protocol is. What is the rule for lunchtime detentions? How long can you reasonably keep pupils in detention? Whom do you need to tell? What about after-school detentions? How much notice must you give parents? Can the child get home safely afterwards? As I said above, there is nothing worse when you are dealing with an awkward child than to make a mistake that results in you being on the back foot when an irate parent rings in!

Always avoid whole-class detentions. We bumped into this area in an earlier section, so let's look at it from a different angle. Remember those hardworking kids who you think you will be able to get in your pocket, who are going to help you with your discipline? You will lose them as well if you keep them in when they haven't done anything wrong, and again when their parents phone to complain; it is a very hard one to justify.

If you do need to detain a child after school, and you have followed all the necessary procedures, make sure you are available to supervise the detention. There is nothing worse when you have a meeting than seeing four or five kids sitting in the corridor outside larking about and having a high old time. All because the teacher had forgotten that they had a meeting, so has sat them in the corridor where they are just messing about.

Contracts

Finally, it may be useful to think of a contract for persistent offenders. Again it is worth your time and effort to go to your word processor and have this ready for when you see the child. It will have their name very formally at the top. It will list the behaviour that the child admits to, e.g. talking in class, interfering with other kids' chances of learning, etc. It will list what the pupil is going to do now, e.g. stop talking, not call out, complete more written work, etc. It will also list what will happen if the contract is broken, e.g. I will have to stay in at dinner, my teacher will tell my family, etc. Then get them to sign it and you sign it. You can give it extra weight by getting your head of department or another colleague to sign it as well. Then keep it in a smart-looking file. Whenever they are in danger of transgressing again, just show them the file. It is usually enough.

There are no doubt an endless variety of strategies for dealing with very difficult pupils. At the end of the day, remember that they still demand that you control them, difficult as they make it for you to do so, and they will give you their total loyalty if you succeed. You are much more likely to succeed if you show them respect and engage them in finding solutions than if you go in gung-ho with a macho swashbuckling style which aims to humiliate them into compliance, but which has a horrible habit of coming back to haunt you when, one way or another, you come face to face with these young people again.

However, when you start to win through, it is one of the most satisfying feelings in the world. Yes, that is another reason why I am a teacher.

I guess when it comes to dealing with very difficult classes and challenging individuals, you have to be at your brilliant best. Your planning, your classroom management, your delivery has to be the best you can do. Like everything else in this game, you need to spend time thinking through what the best strategies for each situation are. It won't just happen! You will need to work at it over a period of time, accepting advice and help from more experienced colleagues.

Bonus story

Thailand. Land of sunshine, beaches, sex tourism and Buddha.[56] And, of course, the marvellously named capital, Bangkok.

In one of the temples sits a golden Buddha. As you know, Buddha is a hefty chap and this statue is no exception. It's a ten-foot tall, solid gold sumo guy. And next to Buddha is an interesting exhibit that attracts much less attention. It's a two-foot thick lump of clay. The exhibits are linked, their story going back thousands of years...

---

[56] I don't want ever to catch you stereotyping!

The original gold statue was housed in an ancient monastery. The monks heard there was a plan afoot to raid the monastery and steal the art and antiques, so they covered the gold Buddha with a two-foot layer of clay. They hoped the robbers would ignore a clay Buddha, worthless as it seemed. Good news and bad news. The good news is that the monks' idea worked and the Buddha was ignored. Bad news, the monks were slaughtered. Whoops!

A few thousand years later a team of archaeologists came across the derelict abbey, saw the giant clay Buddha and thought it would look good in their museum. So they built a wagon and started wheeling it through the jungle. The Buddha statue is a very heavy artefact and one of the wagon wheels gave way, cracking the clay ever so slightly. The team rested for the night while the rain pelted down. One of the guys got up in the night to check on the clay Buddha. He shone his torch and something glinted back at him. You've guessed it; they spent the next day chipping off the two feet of clay to reveal the shiny fella in all his 24-carat glory.

And the bleedin' obvious point? Two-fold. As a teacher we are all a bit like the gold statue. Over the years we get weighed down by responsibility. Life adds layers to us. We've got to be a great parent, a world-class teacher, a decent friend, a loving partner and a half-decent socialite. We go on courses that tell us how to behave, how to safeguard children, how to be emotionally intelligent, how to implement VAK in the classroom and how to ask the right questions at interviews. Layer upon layer is added until, do you know what, we've almost buried our brilliance. There's gold inside folks, but the outside can become heavy and dull. The ethos of this book is to chip away at the stuff that weighs us down, and to reveal our sparkly, shiny, world-class inner-selves. Shine, people, shine!

And there's also gold in them there kids! You don't have to be an alchemist. It's already there. Super-teachers know this, and what makes them 'super' is that they find it!

Part 4

And finally...

A couple of pages where we've pulled everything together. We've run out of Winnie the Pooh quotes so you'll have to make do with something from *Charlotte's Web*, plus a final bonus story about baby monkeys. Enjoy!

Read. Do. Inspire

> *Chin up, chin up. Everyone loves a happy face. Wear it. Have it. It'll brighten up the darkest place. Twinkle. Sparkle. Let a little sunshine in. You'll be on the right side looking on the bright side. Up with your chinny-chin-chin.*
>
> **From Charlotte's Web by E. B White**

Final thoughts. We desperately wanted to avoid a book that was full of jargon. We have avoided attacking the politics of teaching and ranting about all the things that successive governments have got wrong. Too easy! And we most certainly didn't want to produce a turgid tome on the 'theory' of teaching.

We simply wanted to share what, in our experience, is best practice in life and in the classroom. And to write in a style that made you think and (we hope) grin. This final part is a call to action.

You don't work in a factory making widgets. If you fancy doing that, please apply at your local widget factory. On the downside, you'll find that the job involves thirty-nine hours of tedium, doing repetitive work and the pay is £10k less than you're currently on. Oh, and they'll reduce your holidays by ten weeks a year.

But there's an upside. You'll be able to clock off at 5 p.m. and forget about work. No prep, no marking, no parents' evenings and no panic attacks about class 4M.

Alternatively, try your local supermarket. You've had a go at the self-service checkout so maybe you'd like a till all of your own? Flexible hours, double pay on Bank Holidays. Nice uniform. Regular tea breaks. Staff discount.

I guess we're back to life choices. If you weigh up the pros and cons of the widget factory we think, on balance, you'd hate it. Of course, it might be great for a day or a week - no pressure, freedom in the evenings, ability to take holidays out of school term time - but ten years? Or twenty, or thirty?

The supermarket is a novel idea. At least in the short term. But as a career?

You see, you're already doing the best job in the world. Sometimes we lose focus. Sometimes we get ground down by the relentless pace of change and the morbid obesity of 'responsibility'. But, deep down, you already know that you, at your best, can achieve magnificent things in the classroom. You, at your best, are a positive influence on your colleagues. And you, at your best, have the power to connect with young people, enthuse them about your subject and engage them in a lifetime of learning. That's worth a million widgets and a billion Tesco's vouchers!

The sub-heading of this book is 'Read. Do. Inspire.' Reflect on *The Art of Being a Brilliant Teacher* and the lessons within. Some may be new to you. Some stuff you already knew but weren't doing. Some may be a reminder of some of the great habits you already have. Ultimately, it's about being you *at your best!*

> After all, why settle for anything less than being yourself, brilliantly?
>
> **Chris, Gary and Andy**

Final bonus story

How do you catch a baby monkey? Sounds like the start of a joke but, read on, this is true.

First, to catch a baby monkey, you have to go to a place where monkeys live (i.e. the jungle) and dig a hole in the ground. You then put a cage into the hole and place a banana in the cage. You then sit behind a tree and wait. Said monkey will gambol through the forest, see the banana and think, 'yum yum, I like bananas'. The monkey will then reach in and grab the banana. But the monkey can't work out how to get the banana out. Its arm is in the cage, banana grasped tightly, but the banana won't fit through the bars. Picture one very puzzled primate.

The monkey catcher can then simply saunter up to the monkey and capture it. The monkey can see the man approaching and knows it's going to get caught. Yikes! All it has to do is let go of the banana and do a runner. But, here's the rub, the monkey would rather hang on to the banana and get caught.[57]

I guess the final message in this book is just about the most important. We all have habits - some good and some bad. In order to move on we sometimes have to learn to let go of the things that are holding us back. Metaphorically, how many bananas are you holding on to? How many things do you continue to do, through force of habit, that are not serving your best interests?

In the classroom, you might be in the habit of bellowing at 4M. It's not working but you continue to do it.

You might be approaching a certain class with a hardened negativity before they've even entered your classroom. The negativity ain't working, but you continue to do it.

You enjoy having a moan about things in staff meetings and it's draining the people around you. Once again, it's not working, but you continue to do it.

You get home and groan to your other half about how awful you day's been. I think you get the message?

Let go folks. Try something new. Read. Do. Inspire!

---

[57] Cue puzzled looks on your faces as you read this. What on earth is he on about? Monkeys and bananas? What's this got to do with teaching?